# 100
## GREATS

# CELTIC
## FOOTBALL CLUB

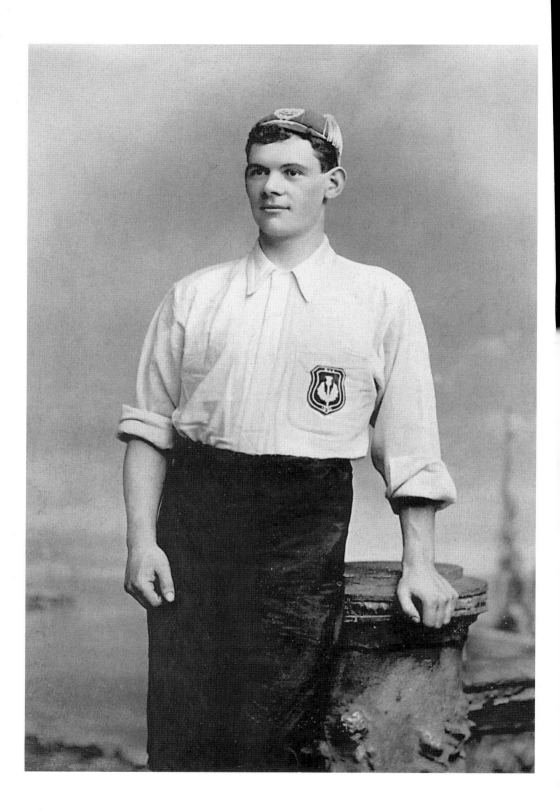

**100 GREATS**

# CELTIC
## FOOTBALL CLUB

COMPILED BY
PAUL LUNNEY

TEMPUS

*Frontispiece:* Great full-back and personality of the 1890s, Dan Doyle.

First published 2005

Tempus Publishing Limited
The Mill, Brimscombe Port,
Stroud, Gloucestershire, GL5 2QG
www.tempus-publishing.com

© Paul Lunney, 2005

The right of Paul Lunney to be identified as the Author
of this work has been asserted in accordance with the
Copyrights, Designs and Patents Act 1988.

British Library Cataloguing in Publication Data.
A catalogue record for this book is available from the British Library.

ISBN 0 7524 2741 5

Typesetting and origination by Tempus Publishing Limited.
Printed in Great Britain.

# Introduction

One of the oldest and truest clichés in football is that the game is all about opinions. It follows, therefore, that the choice by any one supporter of the hundred greatest Celtic players is unlikely to coincide exactly with the choice by any other. So my selection is an entirely personal one and of the great rather than the greatest of the players who have represented the club in first-class matches. Even so, there will be much opportunity for debate.

Celtic Football & Athletic Club has been rich in brilliant purveyors of the beautiful game throughout its glorious history. Indeed, from the very beginning the committee wanted to be a giant in the sport, and did their utmost to obtain the best footballers in the land, to bring honour on the Irish immigrant community of Glasgow. Sadly, Edinburgh's Hibernian fell victim to this ambition, as the infant outfit enticed their young men of star quality to go west and find fame and fortune with Celtic. In compiling this volume, I first thought to include every member of the eight or nine great teams in the club's illustrious history, but the fact soon dawned on me there would be no place for the likes of goalkeeper Willie Miller (1942–50), full-back Dunky MacKay (1958–64) or midfielder John Collins (1990–96), three exceptional talents who unfortunately were at Parkhead during lean periods. Not to include them would have been a major oversight – after all a great Celt is a great Celt, no matter how unsuccessful the team is at the time in question. The names of the 'Bould Bhoys' who just missed out on my final selection are plentiful and far too numerous to list in full, so I'll just take the left-half position at random to give you an example of the standard of player Celtic set: great, yet still unable to get into my golden 100 – Peter Johnstone, John McMaster, Pat McAuley, Joe Baillie, John Clark, Jim Brogan and Derek Whyte. You can see how hard my job was.

The magnificent midfield trio of Lennon, Petrov and Thompson from the current squad deserve a mention as they also just failed to make the cut, but they are Celtic greats nonetheless. I hope you enjoy reading about these Celtic stars of yesteryear, and here's hoping there will be many more wonderful footballers on view in Paradise in the future.

'Sure it's a grand old team to play for.'

Paul Lunney
August 2004

# Acknowledgements

Almost all of the photographs in this book are taken from my own personal collection of memorabilia. However, special mention must be given to the *Scottish Daily Express*, the *Celtic View* and D. Moffat. The front cover photograph, and those of Jackie McNamara and Chris Sutton, are courtesy of D.C. Thomson & Co. Ltd. I would also like to thank Davy Crotty, Derek Taylor, Jack Boyle, James Howarth, Holly Bennion, Rob Sharman and all the staff at Tempus Publishing for making this publication possible.

Lastly a name check must be given to Celtic historians Tom Campbell, Eugene MacBride, Martin O'Connor, David Potter, George Sheridan, Graham McColl and Pat Woods for all their painstaking research on the club over the years. Well done, lads.

Key to Statistics Sections:

The Playres career details with Celtic are self explanatory, however substitute appearances are shown in brackets and are in addition to the full appearances shown.

The other competitions includes the following list of trophies – Glasgow Exhibition Cup (1888), North Eastern Cup, Glasgow League, Inter-City League, Glasgow Exhibition Trophy (1901), British League Cup (1902), Inter-City Midweek League, Belgian War Fund Shield, Navy and Army War Fund Shield, Victory Cup (1919), Lord Provast's Unemployment Cup, Glasgow Dental Hospital Cup, St Vincent de Paul Cup, Empire Exhibition Trophy, all the unofficial wartime competitions, Victory-In-Europe Cup, Victory Cup (1946), St Mungo Cup, Coronation Cup, Friendship Cup, Wolrd Club Championship, Drybrough Cup, Anglo-Scottish Cup and Dubai Cup. Glasgow and Charity Cup games are listed seperately except when the player has competed in Europe; in which case they are included in the Other Competitions section.

*Records not complete.

# 100 Celtic Greats

Davy Adams
Roy Aitken
*Bertie Auld*
Barney Battles
Alec Bennett
Packie Bonner
Tom Boyd
John Browning
Willie Buchan
Tommy Burns
Johnny Campbell
Joe Cassidy
Stevie Chalmers
Bobby Collins
John Collins
George Connelly
Paddy Crerand
Willie Cringan
*Johnny Crum*
*Kenny Dalglish*
Dixie Deans
Jimmy Delaney
Joe Dodds
*Dan Doyle*
Johnny Doyle
*Bobby Evans*
Sean Fallon
Willie Fernie
*Patsy Gallagher*
Chic Geatons
Tommy Gemmell
Peter Grant
*Willie Groves*
Frank Haffey

David Hay
Jimmy Hay
Bobby Hogg
Harry Hood
John Hughes
Mo Johnston
*Jimmy Johnstone*
James Kelly
*Joe Kennaway*
Paul Lambert
*Henrik Larsson*
Bobby Lennox
Willie Loney
Willie Lyon
Malky MacDonald
Dunky MacKay
Murdo MacLeod
Johnny Madden
Willie Maley
Dan McArthur
Andy McAtee
Frank McAvennie
Joe McBride
Brian McClair
Jimmy McColl
Jean McFarlane
Frank McGarvey
Peter McGonagle
Danny McGrain
*Jimmy McGrory*
*Tommy McInally*
Adam McLean
*Sandy McMahon*
Jimmy McMenemy

Alec McNair
Jackie McNamara
*Billy McNeill*
John McPhail
Jimmy McStay
Paul McStay
Willie McStay
Willie Miller
Neil Mochan
Lubo Moravcic
*Bobby Murdoch*
Frank Murphy
Charlie Napier
Charlie Nicholas
Willie Orr
George Paterson
*Bertie Peacock*
Davie Provan
*Jimmy Quinn*
Peter Scarff
Charlie Shaw
Ronnie Simpson
*Peter Somers*
Jock Stein
Chris Sutton
Alec Thomson
*John Thomson*
*Charlie Tully*
Willie Wallace
Jock Weir
Peter Wilson
Sunny Jim Young

The top twenty players appear here in italics. Each of these Celtic stars are allocated two pages instead of the usual one.

# Davy Adams
Goalkeeper 1902-1912

| | Appearances | Shut-outs |
|---|---|---|
| League | 247 | 102 |
| Scottish Cup | 43 | 24 |
| Glasgow Cup | 27 | 11 |
| Charity Cup | 14 | 4 |
| Other Competitions | 17 | 3 |
| TOTAL | 349 | 142 |

Big Davy Adams was the last line of Celtic's first truly great side (1904–10), and represented Scotland at junior level with Dunipace before arriving at Parkhead midway through the 1902/03 term.

He was a colossus of a custodian (only the legendary 'Fatty' Foulkes of that era seemed bigger), yet was surprisingly adept at saving low shots for such a huge man. After some initial shaky performances, Adams soon settled and became respected as one of the better goalkeepers in the Scottish League.

He won numerous club honours, including six successive Championship medals, but never received recognition at full international level. One explanation offered was that the players immediately in front of him were so secure that he was seldom called into action; and, indeed, Adams often complained of getting cold through inactivity behind such a well-drilled defence. At the beginning of the 1906/07 campaign, Davy suffered a badly cut hand playing in a benefit game at Ibrox for Rangers star Finlay Speedie. The mishap was caused through a nail which had been inserted in a goalpost for a five-a-side tournament during a sports meeting and had not been removed. Adams, in making a save, lacerated his hand. Rangers kindly loaned the Celts their reserve Tom Sinclair in the meantime.

Adams loved repartee and on one memorable occasion when McLeod was bitching on to him after conceding a soft goal, Adams began to get irritated as the full-back kept going on about the mistake. MacLeod: 'How the hell did you lose that ball?' Adams: 'Shut up! I know where the ball is. I havnae lost it. It's in the net!'

His swansong was the 1911 Scottish Cup, which Celtic lifted without conceding a goal throughout the competition. He continued to play on till December of that year, but eye trouble forced his retirement a few months later. Big Davy was the last Celtic 'keeper to appear in the hoops and the first to wear a distinguishable yellow jersey. Little is known of his subsequent life until he died in Edinburgh on 29 November 1948, aged sixty-five.

# Roy Aitken
Half-back/midfielder 1975-1990

| | Appearances | Goals |
|---|---|---|
| League | 483 | 40 |
| Scottish Cup | 55 | 4 |
| League Cup | 82 (2) | 6 |
| Europe | 47 | 5 |
| Other Competitions | 15 | 1 |
| TOTAL | 682 (2) | 56 |

'That boy will play for Scotland.' So said Jock Stein after watching the energetic thirteen-year-old Aitken star for Celtic Boys' Club. However, it didn't take a genius of the Big Man's magnitude to see that the determined teenager possessed all the skills and fighting qualities needed to make it in the top flight.

An Ayrshire lad, Roy captained his school team, St Andrew's Academy, Saltcoats, to victory in the Scottish Schools Basketball Cup Final of 1973, and also represented Great Britain at that sport. Roy's quieter moments saw him gain a piano-playing diploma from the London Royal Academy of Music, but these achievements proved a mere sideline to his forthcoming prowess as a footballer. A Celtic debutant at the age of sixteen against Stenhousemuir in September 1975, he established himself as a first-team regular during the club's 1976/77 double-winning campaign. As a wholehearted, hard-working half-back with a never-say-die attitude, he won every major domestic honour possible at Parkhead. Unfortunately, his some-times enthusiastic physical approach led to five red cards being brandished during an illustrious career. These early baths included the first time he was given the captain's armband as an over-eager and naïve nineteen-year-old in a Scottish Cup tie against Kilmarnock at Rugby Park in 1978, and the 1984 final clash with Aberdeen.

Thankfully, the highs far outweigh the lows and Aitken's spirited performances on the football field had an inspirational effect on those around him. The 1979 League clincher against Rangers and the 1985 Scottish Cup final victory over Dundee United are two cases in point, when Aitken brought the Bhoys back from the brink of defeat to triumphant glory. He skippered the Celts' centenary celebrations in 1988 with a League and cup double, and returned to Hampden the next year to retain the 'Blue Riband' against arch-rivals Rangers.

'The Bear' departed Paradise for Newcastle United in January 1990 for £500,000, and not surprisingly a lot of Celtic's heart went with him. He cost St Mirren £225,000 in August 1991 as player-coach, and then moved on to Aberdeen in the summer of 1992 for £100,000. At Pittodrie he subsequently became assistant manager, acting manager and then finally manager in May 1995, with a League Cup final success being registered the following season against Dundee. He has recently been part of David O'Leary's backroom staff at Leeds and is now at Aston Villa.

# Bertie Auld

Outside left 1955-1961, Midfielder 1965-1971

| | Appearances | Goals |
|---|---|---|
| League | 167 (9) | 53 |
| Scottish Cup | 26 (2) | 8 |
| League Cup | 42 (5) | 20 |
| Europe | 20 (2) | 1 |
| Other Competitions | 16 | 7 |
| TOTAL | 271 (18) | 89 |

When Bertie Auld joined Celtic from Maryhill Harp in 1955, Charlie Tully recalled that he was neither nervous nor over-awed: 'I noticed Bertie wasn't a bit shy as some young fellows are in a new club. He was full of confidence. I remember he used to lark about in a jokey cap and before I knew it he was calling me "Daddy".'

His splendid performances for the Hoops as a strong-shooting left-winger gained him international recognition by the Scottish selectors, and after playing in the Inter-League game against England, there followed a Scotland tour of Jutland, Holland and Portugal. However, his temperament came into question when he became only the second Scotland player to be ordered off (the first being Billy Steel *v* Austria in 1951) in the match with Holland on 27 May 1959.

As an aggressive, fearless forward with a short fuse, Auld failed to endear himself to the club chairman and strict disciplinarian Bob Kelly, and in 1961 he moved to Birmingham City for £15,000. At St Andrews he played in the first leg of the 1961 Fairs Cup final versus AS Roma, and won a Football League Cup winner's tankard with the Blues in 1963.

Another two years passed before coach Sean Fallon persuaded Chairman Kelly that he should travel south to bring back Bertie, and so the outstanding midfield partnership of Murdoch and Auld was born. Fallon said: 'We were playing mile-a-minute stuff at the time and he complemented Bobby Murdoch by slowing things down. He could take two or three people out of the game with a pass.' Bertie amusingly renamed the pair 'McKellar and Watt' after the link men.

A wage cut of £5 a week never worried Auld, and he immediately showed he had lost none of his savvy, as the following tale illustrates. Celtic were playing Kilmarnock and the teams were wearing armbands. They were the tie-on type and Bertie's came loose and fluttered to the ground just as the ball went out of play for a throw-in to Celtic at the corner-flag. He politely asked the linesman to tie it back on and the official promptly put his flag on the grass and began his task. Meanwhile, Bertie began working the ball into the corner arc with his feet. As the linesman bent down to pick up his flag, Bertie took a corner. When the linesman looked up to see the ball curving high into the penalty area, he knew what had happened, but the referee hadn't twigged and the fans were hysterical.

Auld's brace of goals in the 1965 Scottish Cup final win over Dunfermline Athletic gave birth to

Bertie Auld scores the only goal of the 1969/70 League Cup final at Hampden against St Johnstone.

the Stein era at Parkhead. Cunning and confident with his aggression lurking near the surface, he became an integral part of the side which swept the board of domestic honours and the European Cup in 1967, and it was the fierce and wily Bertie who destroyed Fiorentina in Paradise three years later to set up the 'Battle of Britain' European Cup semi-final with Leeds United.

In May 1971, he left for Hibs, and when they faced Middlesbrough in a pre-season friendly at Easter Road the press were full of the forthcoming Auld/Stiles clash. During the game Nobby Stiles fouled him and broke his collar bone in the process, but Bertie refused to leave the field. His team-mate Eric Stevenson recalled: 'A few minutes later there was a 50-50 ball and Bertie let Stiles dive in and was waiting for him. As the dust settled Stiles was carried off screaming to the sanctuary of the dressing room. You just didn't mess with Bertie.'

He subsequently managed Partick Thistle, Hibernian, Hamilton Accies and Dumbarton.

# Barney Battles

Full-back 1895-1897, Half-back 1898-1904

|  | Appearances | Goals |
|---|---|---|
| League | 110 | 6 |
| Scottish Cup | 26 | 0 |
| Glasgow Cup | 20 | 0 |
| Charity Cup | 16 | 2 |
| Other Competitions | 37 | 0 |
| TOTAL | 209 | 8 |

Brave and bustling Barney Battles moved to Midlothian from Springburn when still a boy and played his early football in the Linlithgow area. He joined Hearts in 1894 and Celtic the following year. A dominant defender of heavyweight proportions, whether at full- or half-back, Battles was totally committed, being both enthusiastic and fearless. Although he lacked pace, his excellent anticipation and finely judged interventions more than compensated for this one defect. Big Barney made his Celtic debut in a 2–1 away win at Dundee on 10 August 1895, and appropriately signed for the Dark Blues after a brief spell with Liverpool in May 1897. He rejoined the Bhoys in October 1898, and so impressed the Scottish selectors with his consistent performances that he starred in all three Home Internationals of 1901.

Battles gained League Championship medals with Hearts (1895) and Celtic (1896), and two Scottish Cup winner's badges at Parkhead (1899, 1900), and also represented the Scottish League and Glasgow v. Sheffield in 1902.

Transferred in the summer of 1904 to Kilmarnock, Barney went down with influenza after playing in a League match at Ibrox on 21 January 1905. He felt well enough to watch a Scottish Cup tie against Beith the next week, but the flu developed into pneumonia and he died suddenly at home in Glasgow's Gallowgate on 9 February 1905, at the age of thirty. A reported 40,000 people lined the route to Dalbeth cemetery to pay tribute to this hugely popular player. Battles had a wife and young daughters and was probably unaware that his wife was pregnant again. This child, a boy named after Barney, would emulate the father he never knew by growing up to play for Hearts and Scotland.

In 1966, Barney Junior presented his father's 1895/96 Championship gold medal to Celtic manager Jock Stein.

| | Appearances | Goals |
|---|---|---|
| League | 125 | 49 |
| Scottish Cup | 26 | 6 |
| Glasgow Cup | 14 | 6 |
| Charity Cup | 8 | 5 |
| Other Competitions | 13 | 7 |
| TOTAL | 186 | 73 |

A member of arguably Celtic's greatest ever forward line (Bennett, McMenemy, Quinn, Somers and Hamilton), Alec joined Celtic from Rutherglen Glencairn in 1903 and renewed his outstanding attacking partnership with Jimmy McMenemy, which had been so rewarding for the junior side.

Slight in build, Bennett created havoc in the final third of the pitch with an array of attributes which included great speed and trickery on the ball allied with an ability to score important goals. Initially a centre forward, he made way for Jimmy Quinn and moved out on to the wing, where he became an elusive and often brilliant outside right. Bennett certainly set the heather on fire, and after being a hat-trick hero as the Celts walloped St Mirren 5–2 in the Glasgow Charity Cup final of 1903, Alec made his international debut for Scotland during his first full season at Parkhead (a 1–1 draw against Wales in Dundee on 12 March 1904). He won four Championship medals with Celtic (1905–08) and two Scottish Cup winner's medals (1907, 1908), before joining Rangers as a free agent

under an agreement of a £50 release clause. Adored by the Celtic supporters, one fan penetrated the pavilion, enquired which were Bennett's boots and began to extract the laces. He winked to 'Icicle' McNair and proclaimed: 'I'll keep these. Just a wee souvenir.'

Bennett won further honours with the Ibrox club, received eleven Scotland caps and also represented the Scottish League on ten occasions. During the First World War he played for Dumbarton and ended his playing career at Albion Rovers in 1920/21. Alec subsequently managed Third Lanark and Clydebank and wrote a column for the *Daily Record*. He died on 9 January 1940, aged fifty-eight. His grandson, Sandy Carmichael, was a famous Scotland rugby international.

# Packie Bonner

Goalkeeper 1978-1996

| | Appearances | Shut-outs |
|---|---|---|
| **League** | 483 | 179 |
| **Scottish Cup** | 55 | 35 |
| **League Cup** | 64 | 26 |
| **Europe** | 40 | 15 |
| **Other Competitions** | 7 | 2 |
| **TOTAL** | 649 | 257 |

'Packie' Bonner from County Donegal was Jock Stein's last signing for Celtic, on 14 May 1978, and had previously kept goal for Leicester City in the FA Youth Cup. Bonner recalled:'I was so excited. I remember Jock Stein giving me the £100 and saying "now give your mum some of that."' He arrived at Parkhead from Keadue Rovers and appropriately made his home debut on St Patrick's Day 1979 in a 2–1 league win over Motherwell. He became Celts' established last line after an inspired display in Danny McGrain's testimonial match against Manchester United in August 1980. The alert and attentive Bonner's athletic leaps and cat-like agility made one believe that he had springs in his heels as he flew through the air to push a ball round the post or over the bar.

'Packie' won the first of his 80 international caps for the Republic of Ireland against Poland in 1981, and he is still Celtic's most capped player. Sadly he missed the 1988 Scottish Cup final victory over Dundee United due to injury, but went on to have a magnificent European Championship that summer in Germany, which included a breathtaking stop from Gary Lineker in the defeat of England.

A couple of years later he proved to be Eire's saviour in the World Cup Finals penalty shoot-out against Romania. Afterwards His Holiness Pope John Paul II told Bonner: 'I know you are the goalkeeper – I used to play in that position.'

At thirty-five, the big Donegal man crowned a glorious goalkeeping career at Paradise with a clean sheet in the 1995 Scottish Cup final triumph over Airdrie. He holds the record for most appearances between the posts for the club and Celtic faced the Republic of Ireland in his testimonial match in 1991. 'Packie' was subsequently a coach at Parkhead and later Reading, and is currently the goalkeeping coach for his country. His twin brother Denis played for Sligo Rovers.

# Tom Boyd
Full-back 1992-2003

| | Appearances | Goals |
|---|---|---|
| League | 296 (10) | 2 |
| Scottish Cup | 31 (3) | 0 |
| League Cup | 31 (2) | 0 |
| Europe | 33 (1) | 0 |
| Other Competitions | 0 | 0 |
| TOTAL | 391 (16) | 2 |

When all is said and done, the lasting impression of Tom Boyd's career with Celtic is that of a too cautious approach. 'He was a defender!' I hear you cry. However, the fact remains that when he starred for Motherwell or in Scotland's dark blue jersey Boyd played like a world beater – a sort of reincarnation of Danny McGrain bounding up and down the flank with a terrific turn of speed – but in the Hoops he never really showed the same kind of adventurous spirit. Nonetheless he did his job with credible reliability and received a testimonial against Manchester United in 2001 after ten seasons of sterling service to the cause.

An S form signing for Motherwell by assistant boss and ex-Celt Frank Connor, he began his playing career at Fir Park on a YTS and rose to the heady heights of being only the second skipper in the club's history to lift the Scottish Cup. Indeed, he won the Cup, moved to Chelsea for 'Well's all-time record fee of £800,000 and got married all within the space of eleven days in May 1991.

Tommy joined Celtic on 6 February 1992 in a straight swap for Tony Cascarino – a centre forward who failed to make his mark at Parkhead – and gave competent performances throughout his period in Paradise. In 1997 he gained the team captaincy from the recently retired Paul McStay and immediately led Celtic to Coca-Cola Cup and League Championship triumphs. He won 72 caps (66 with Celtic) and captained Scotland as they beat Latvia at Celtic Park to qualify for the World Cup Finals in France. A dedicated professional with a long distinguished career, Tom Boyd received an MBE in the Queen's Birthday Honours list in summer 2002 for services to football, and retired the following year.

# John Browning

Left-winger 1912-1919

|  | Appearances | Goals |
|---|---|---|
| **League** | 210 | 65 |
| **Scottish Cup** | 7 | 2 |
| **Glasgow Cup** | 9 | 4 |
| **Charity Cup** | 14 | 2 |
| **Other Competitions** | 9 | 1 |
| **TOTAL** | 249 | 74 |

'**S**on of the Rock' John 'Smiler' Browning was a strong, sturdy winger with a straight-forward, forceful attacking flair which realised plenty of goals. In his seven seasons with Celtic, he scored an average of a goal every three games, including 15 in the 1914/15 campaign. Browning loved to cut inside from the left flank and have a pop at goal, and was equally effective as a provider with pinpoint accurate crosses and corner kicks.

On 28 February 1914, Johnny made his only appearance for Scotland in a goalless draw against Wales at Parkhead. It was a day when Celtic lost 1–0 at Falkirk, hardly a surprising outcome considering that fellow Bhoys, Dodds and McMenemy, were also fielded for Scotland

that afternoon. Browning represented the Scottish League on two occasions, was selected for the annual Glasgow *v.* Sheffield fixture in 1914, and netted a brace of goals in the 1914 Scottish Cup final replay win over Hibernian.

The dressing room comedian and Harry Lauder impersonator, 'Smiler' started his career with Glasgow Perthshire and moved south to Chelsea in June 1919, ironically playing his last game for the Hoops against his former club Vale of Leven in a Victory Cup match on 1 March – bowing out with a goal in Celts' 2–0 win. However, he didn't have a happy time at Stamford Bridge, having suffered injury before being freed by the Pensioners. Johnny went to Dumbarton and Leven again before hanging up his boots. In 1924, he and ex-Ranger Archie Kyle were found guilty of attempting to bribe Bo'ness player Peter Brown in a pub in Glasgow's Dundas Street: both men were sentenced to sixty days' hard labour.

A baker by trade, his son John junior played at Bridgeton Waverley, Dunoon Athletic and for Liverpool from 1934 to 1939.

# Willie Buchan
Inside forward 1933-1937

|  | Appearances | Goals |
|---|---|---|
| League | 121 | 49 |
| Scottish Cup | 13 | 8 |
| Glasgow Cup | 9 | 1 |
| Charity Cup | 7 | 3 |
| Other Competitions | 0 | 0 |
| TOTAL | 150 | 61 |

A footballer of finesse, Willie Buchan began his long career with Cowie Juveniles and signed for Celtic from the local side Grange Rovers in January 1933. Lithe and graceful, he possessed all the attributes which make such a quality performer: he was a deft passer, a mazy dribbler and had the knack of scoring important goals.

He was renowned as a penalty taker – with consummate skill he would take a long run up and use his body swerve to deceive and wrong-foot the goalkeeper. Alas, his stay in Paradise should have been longer. Talking about his transfer to Blackpool in November 1937 for £10,000, Buchan said: 'Willie Maley asked me to come and see him in the Bank Restaurant. The Blackpool manager was already there and the deal had already been concluded. The way things were put to me, it seemed I had no choice in the matter. It was a great disappointment as I was enjoying playing for Celtic. In those days, players who had been in the team for five years were paid a benefit of £600. Since then I am led to believe that my transfer took place to pay the benefits of all the players that had broken through in the early times.'

Willie scored the winner in the 1937 Scottish Cup final, represented the Scottish League twice and played for Scotland against England in the unofficial wartime international of 1943.

Buchan made guest appearances for a number of clubs during the war, including Manchester United, Manchester City, Bristol City and Bath City. He cost Hull City their record fee of £5,000 in January 1948, converted two penalties on his debut and helped the Tigers win the Division Three (North) Championship in 1949. Buchan then played for Gateshead and managed Coleraine, before ending his career with East Stirlingshire.

On returning to his native Grangemouth in 1954, Willie was employed as a process worker at ICI, and kept himself fit on retirement with leisure pursuits such as cycling and ballroom dancing. The last of the 1936 League Champions, Willie Buchan died on 6 July 2003, aged eighty-eight.

# Tommy Burns

Inside left 1975-1989

| | Appearances | Goals |
|---|---|---|
| **League** | 324 (32) | 52 |
| **Scottish Cup** | 38 (5) | 12 |
| **League Cup** | 70 (1) | 15 |
| **Europe** | 32 (3) | 4 |
| **Other Competitions** | 16 | 2 |
| **TOTAL** | 480 (41) | 85 |

One of Scotland's most naturally gifted and creative midfielders in the 1980s, Tommy Burns played for Eastercraigs and Maryhill FC before making the grade with Celtic. Born within a free-kick of Paradise, Tommy made his home debut as a substitute for Paul Wilson in a 1–2 defeat from Dundee on 19 April 1975.

A polished performer at inside left, he also occasionally occupied the left-back berth to good effect. Burns's early days saw turbulent times, and it seemed that his clashes with authority would stunt his progress. In one eighteen-month period he received three red cards.

Amazingly, his attitude turned full-circle and he emerged a true sportsman, never retaliating, even in the face of some intense provocation, notably after being punched by Kienast of Rapid Vienna and Hearts' John Robertson. He collected all the domestic honours, and made

eight appearances for Scotland, winning his last cap after a gap of five years, when he substituted for Neil Simpson against England at Wembley in May 1988.

Tommy affectionately donated his boots to the Jungle after his last game for Celtic against Ajax in December 1989 and joined Kilmarnock that same month. He tried his luck in the 'hot seat' at Parkhead, but like Brady and Barnes was never manager material – humiliation from lower league sides Raith Rovers and Falkirk only emphasised the point. Tommy has since coached at Newcastle United, been boss at Reading and was recently surprisingly promoted from Youth Development Officer at Celtic Park to first-team coach by new manager Gordon Strachan. Many felt he should also have been sacked or resigned when Berite Vogts was dismissed as national team boss, but Walter Smith decided to keep him on as an assistant.

'Kings may be blest / But Tam was Glorious' wrote another Burns. Legions of Celtic supporters will agree with the Scottish bard's sentiments.

| | Appearances | Goals |
|---|---|---|
| League | 169 | 87 |
| Scottish Cup | 46 | 27 |
| Glasgow Cup | 39 | 32 |
| Charity Cup | 24 | 14 |
| Other Competitions | 38 | 27 |
| TOTAL | 316 | 187 |

A lanky and fearfully lean youngster when he signed for Celtic from Benburb in 1890, Possil boy Johnny Campbell fattened out to become a strong, versatile forward who possessed a powerful shot and who once claimed 12 goals in a reserve game for Celts Colts. He formed a devastating left-wing partnership with Sandy McMahon and played a full part in the first years of Celtic's rise to greatness before being lured south to Aston Villa in May 1895 by an offer of £4 a week wages.

His 27 goals in season 1895/96 for the Villans made him the top scorer in Britain. Campbell then put Villa well on their way to winning the League and Cup double in 1896/97. He opened the scoring in the FA Cup final against Everton at Crystal Palace on 10 April 1897 with a deceptive, swerving shot from 25 yards, and topped that feat the following week by converting the first-ever goal at Villa Park against Blackburn Rovers with a solo effort worthy of the occasion.

He returned to Paradise in 1897 after scoring 43 goals in 63 League and FA Cup games for the Birmingham outfit at centre forward. Johnny Campbell collected many honours, which included League and FA Cup winner's medals on both sides of the border, and a

dozen international caps for Scotland. He also represented the Scottish League four times and starred for Glasgow against Sheffield on three occasions; he is the one and only ex-Celt to win a League Championship medal with Third Lanark in 1904.

Johnny was a Scottish representative of the Players' Union and later in life he ran a successful business in Glasgow. He was described by Willie Maley as 'a gentleman of aldermanic proportions'. Campbell owned a public house in London Road, appropriately named the Villa Bar. He died on 2 December 1947, aged seventy-five.

# Joe Cassidy
Inside left/Centre forward 1913-1924

|  | Appearances | Goals |
|---|---|---|
| **League** | 189 | 94 |
| **Scottish Cup** | 15 | 13 |
| **Glasgow Cup** | 10 | 3 |
| **Charity Cup** | 12 | 5 |
| **Other Competitions** | 5 | 1 |
| **TOTAL** | 231 | 116 |

A stylish schemer in attack, Joe Cassidy was a mere slip of a lad when he arrived at Parkhead from Vale of Clyde during the 1912/13 season. He went on loan to Ayr United in 1914 to gain experience before military service in the Black Watch during the First World War interrupted his football career. In November 1918 Trooper Cassidy won the Military Medal. On his return from France he became a good all-round forward, who rapidly established himself as a brilliant striker. Originally an inside forward, his move to centre was due solely to the vacancy created by Tommy McInally's departure to Third Lanark in 1922. Cassidy responded to his new role by finishing as Celts' top marksman in three consecutive seasons (1921/22, 1922/23 and 1923/24), and even today his 11 goals in the 1923 Scottish Cup competition are a club record – and will take some beating.

At Ibrox on Ne'erday 1921 he netted both goals to give Celtic a famous 2–0 victory over arch-rivals Rangers, and one brake charabanc legend gloriously read 'Cassidy 2 Undefeated Rangers 0'. Deadly footwork and precise heading ability made him a sought-after commodity, and subsequent travels took him to several clubs. In turn he played for Bolton Wanderers (August 1924 for £4,500), Cardiff City (October 1925 £3,500), Dundee (August 1926), Clyde (summer 1928), Ballymena (1929), Morton and Dundalk. A measure of Cassidy's transient nature can be gleamed from the fact that his first four children were born in Scotland, England, Wales and Ireland. Joe's honours included four caps for Scotland, three Scottish League appearances, a Championship medal (1922) and a Scottish Cup winner (1923). While with Ballymena he represented the Irish League twice and won an Irish Cup medal (1929). 'Have boots will travel' Joe Cassidy died on 23 July 1949, aged fifty-two.

# Stevie Chalmers
Forward 1959-1971

| | Appearances | Goals |
|---|---|---|
| League | 253 (10) | 156 |
| Scottish Cup | 45 (2) | 29 |
| League Cup | 57 (3) | 31 |
| Europe | 37 (1) | 13 |
| Other Cups | 29 | 11 |
| TOTAL | 421 (16) | 240 |

Lisbon hero Steve Chalmers was a manager's dream forward: lean and speedy. He could be relied on to give his all for the entire duration of every match. A refreshingly direct footballer with no pretensions towards embroidery, Chalmers was razor-sharp and intelligent and, no matter how big the opponent, he never shirked from physical contact if there was any chance of reaching the ball.

Born on Boxing Day 1936, Stevie began his career with Kirkintilloch Rob Roy in 1953. Unfortunately, while there he was in hospital for six months and out of the game for a year due to meningitis. He moved on to Ashfield in 1956 and starred for Scotland at junior level before coming to Parkhead in February 1959, and he remained a mainstay of the side throughout the 1960s. Chalmers collected five full international caps, scoring in a 1–1 draw against Brazil at Hampden in 1966, a game in which he received the prized possession of Pele's jersey.

One of his finest moments came in the European Cup semi-final in Prague when, as Celts' only forward, he covered every blade of grass in his opponents' half. And then in the final he steered Murdoch's shot past Inter's Sarti to guarantee himself immortality.

The swansong arrived with a beautiful banana shot which deceived Norrie Martin and demolished Rangers 4–0 in the Scottish Cup final of 1969. After suffering a broken leg in the 1969/70 League Cup final win over St Johnstone, he found it difficult to regain his place and joined Morton in 1971. He moved to Partick Thistle the following year when he owned a licensed grocers in the Maryhill district and subsequently worked for the Celtic Pools.

A keen photographer and golfer, his father played alongside Jimmy McGrory at Clydebank in the 1920s, while his son Paul made a few appearances for Celtic in the mid-1980s. Stevie Chalmers is one of the club's greatest ever goalscorers.

# Bobby Collins
Forward 1949-1958

| | Appearances | Goals |
|---|---|---|
| League | 220 | 81 |
| Scottish Cup | 38 | 10 |
| League Cup | 62 | 26 |
| Glasgow Cup | 17 | 5 |
| Charity Cup | 9 | 0 |
| Other Competitions | 8 | 3 |
| TOTAL | 354 | 124 |

The 'Wee Barra' with the heart of a lion, Bobby Collins was seventeen, working as a shoemaker in Glasgow and playing for Pollok Juniors, when Everton showed an interest. However, he chose Celtic instead and made a splendid debut at Parkhead in a 3–2 League Cup win over Rangers on 13 August 1949.

A strong, energetic forward who could dribble, shoot and pass to a high standard, he allied these skills to his natural enthusiasm and made himself a firm favourite with the fans, who also nicknamed him 'Lester' after jockey Lester Piggott. His size 4 boots were amongst the smallest in first-class soccer, yet they packed an astonishingly fierce shot.

International recognition beckoned when he was first picked by Scotland in April 1950 to play against Switzerland at Hampden, but he strained a leg in a friendly fixture and missed the game. However, the following autumn, he did collect the first of 31 full caps when Scotland beat Wales 3–1 on 21 October 1950. With Celts

he represented the Scottish League 16 times, and won Championship (1954), Scottish Cup (1951) and League Cup (1956/57, 1957/58) winner's medals.

He ironically transferred to Everton in September 1958 for £23,500, and moved to Leeds United for £25,000 in March 1962. His combative genius in midfield helped transform the Yorkshiremen from a mediocre Second Division side into a powerful force in the First Division. In 1965 he was the first Scot to be elected Footballer of the Year in England, and was also recalled to the Scotland team after a long absence.

Collins came back marvellously after breaking a thigh in Leeds' first European tie later that year, and subsequently led Bury to promotion into the Second Division.

He had a short spell back in Scottish football with Morton, was player-coach in Australia and then starred for Shamrock Rovers before ending his career at Oldham Athletic. Wee Bobby has since been manager of Huddersfield Town, Hull City and Barnsley, and whilst boss at Guiseley he shared a testimonial with John Charles in April 1988 in honour of his Leeds days. He left the game to work in the wholesale fashion business and also worked as a chauffeur at Leeds University garage before retirement.

|  | Appearances | Goals |
|---|---|---|
| League | 211 (6) | 47 |
| Scottish Cup | 21 | 3 |
| League Cup | 22 | 3 |
| Europe | 13 | 1 |
| Other Competitions | 0 | 0 |
| TOTAL | 267 (6) | 54 |

The outstanding talent, John Collins had the misfortune to play for Celtic during one of the worst periods in the club's history. That notwithstanding, his brilliant Brazilian-style free-kick goals for the Hoops at Ibrox against Rangers will long live in the memory.

A hard working, left-sided midfielder with delicate skills and a venomous shot, John Angus Paul Collins made the grade with the capital greens Hibernian in 1984, and cost Celtic a cool £1 million on 12 July 1990. Ironically, he had previously played for Celtic Boys' Club, who allegedly let him leave because they were not willing to meet his travelling expenses from the Borders. Johnny was born at Galashiels on 31 January 1968, and his boundless energy, allied to his creative dribbles and passes, saw him capped 58 times for Scotland before he declined to represent his country again in an international after the 1998 World Cup finals in France.

A Scottish Cup winner with the Bhoys in 1995, he arranged a move to AS Monaco in the summer of 1996 (on the freedom-of-contract Bosman ruling) said to be worth some £2.5 million over three years. With Collins in the engine-room, the Principality won the French League Championship in 1997 and reached the European Cup semi-final the following year. He scored from the penalty spot in the opening game of the 1998 World Cup finals against the holders Brazil before moving back to Great Britain. Former Rangers boss Walter Smith, who could only sit and admire Collins' ability and free-kick expertise at Ibrox, paid £2.5 million to take him to Everton on 7 August 1998, but tragedy struck when a niggling injury hindered his performances and eventually forced him to undergo surgery midway through the 1998/99 campaign. John recovered and signed for Premiership-bound Fulham in July 2000 for £2 million.

# George Connelly
Utility 1968-1975

| | Appearances | Goals |
|---|---|---|
| League | 129 (7) | 5 |
| Scottish Cup | 24 (1) | 2 |
| League Cup | 60 (3) | 4 |
| Europe | 28 (2) | 2 |
| Other Competitions | 15 | 0 |
| TOTAL | 256 (13) | 13 |

George Connelly's presence first came to light in January 1966, when as a teenage protégé on the club's grounds staff he delighted the crowd in the pre-match entertainment for Celts' European Cup Winners' Cup quarter-final tie with a quite brilliant exhibition of 'keepy-uppy'. His average was an incredible 2,000 non-stop.

While playing for Tulliallan Thistle he was recommended to Jock Stein, then boss of Dunfermline, but George had his heart set on Celtic. He bided his time in the Reserves with 'Quality Street' kids like McGrain, Hay, Macari and Dalglish until breaking into the first team on a regular basis around 1970.

Connelly made the most of his big break-through in the 1969 Scottish Cup final 4–0 win over Rangers. With the game on a knife-edge at 1–0, he proved instrumental in effectively ending the contest with two goals in one minute just before half-time. First George intercepted a short pass and prodded the ball through to Lennox, who ran on to score. He then dispossessed Rangers captain John Greig at the corner of his own penalty area and nonchalantly strolled around goalkeeper Martin before tapping the ball into an empty net to make it 3–0. In 1970 he netted the only goal of the European Cup semi-final first leg at Leeds, and also played a blinder in the return at Hampden, yet was surprisingly dropped to the bench for the final against Feyenoord.

Big George always excited the fans with his intelligent ball distribution, excellent reading of the game and skilful attacks from defence, and was once described as Scotland's Franz Beckenbauer. It was sad, then, that he should go on to endure a career punctuated by walk-outs and upheavals because the pressure of being a top player proved too heavy a burden. Nominated Scotland's Player of the Year in 1973, he received two international caps before the troubles began. A broken leg against Basle in 1974 essentially ended his career with Celtic.

A stint at Falkirk failed, and he returned to the juniors to play out his days with Sauchie. For the faithful standing on the slopes of Paradise, it was a heartfelt loss. No more would they admire the stylish subtlety and silky skills from a star of infinite grace.

# Pat Crerand
Right-half 1958-1963

| | Appearances | Goals |
|---|---|---|
| League | 91 | 5 |
| Scottish Cup | 14 | 1 |
| League Cup | 13 | 1 |
| Europe | 2 | 1 |
| Other Competitions | 12 | 2 |
| TOTAL | 132 | 10 |

Gorbals born and bred, Paddy Crerand joined Celtic from Duntocher Hibs in 1957. Unfortunately his period at Parkhead was barren of major domestic honours, except for a Charity Cup winner's medal in 1960.

Crerand perfected his passing skills through constant practice, and such dedication paid dividends as he went on to collect 16 caps for Scotland. However, he was sent off in Czechoslovakia for retaliation during a World Cup qualifying match, and also while playing for Celtic at the Falkirk fives. Those dismissals did little to enhance his relationship with the disciplinarian chairman Bob Kelly. Things came to a head after the 1963 Ne'erday game at Ibrox against Rangers, when a flare-up with coach Sean Fallon resulted in Crerand's name never again featuring on a Celtic team sheet.

The following month, on the recommendation of Denis Law, he went to Manchester United for £56,000. Paddy learned of the move only after it had been concluded, with manager McGrory called in only to formalise the transaction. Crerand recalled: 'I was courting at the time, and we were at the seven o'clock Mass on a Sunday evening at St Francis's Church in Glasgow. I came back after Mass to my mother's house and there was a little guy there, Jim Rodgers, who worked for the *Daily Express*. He said, "You're going to Manchester United."

I was just totally amazed. Nobody had asked me what I thought. It was never a case of "Do you want to go to Manchester United?" – just "You're going". And I had to get the information about it from a newspaper man. "Yes," he said, "Matt Busby's been up. He's done the deal with Bob Kelly. You're going."' Manchester United soon established themselves as England's top team with Crerand in the side and he subsequently became coach and assistant manager at Old Trafford.

In 1976 Celtic wanted a new assistant to Jock Stein but United boss Tommy Docherty would not endorse Pat as a candidate. He managed Northampton Town from July 1976 to January 1977. On leaving football he became a PR officer for a Manchester engineering company and a pub landlord at the Park Hotel, Altrincham.

Centre half 1917-1923

| | Appearances | Goals |
|---|---|---|
| League | 203 | 9 |
| Scottish Cup | 12 | 1 |
| Glasgow Cup | 15 | 1 |
| Charity Cup | 9 | 0 |
| Other Competitions | 7 | 0 |
| TOTAL | 246 | 11 |

An effective pivot and brilliant captain of Celtic, Willie Cringan was born in Muirkirk, Ayrshire, on 15 May 1890, and joined Sunderland from Douglas Water Thistle in the summer of 1910. He played in the FA Cup final of 1913 at Crystal Palace before the Wearsiders closed down for the duration of the First World War. Willie then worked down the pit for the war effort, went on loan to Wishaw Thistle in August 1915, and signed for Ayr United on a temporary transfer in January 1916. He played as a guest for Celtic in a 2–0 Charity Cup win over Rangers at Ibrox on 12 May 1917, and was ultimately purchased for £600 in September 1917. He was a resilient and reliable centre half, 'whose brilliance was undimmed in spite of being on the short side [5ft 8in] for the position'.

Cringan won a Championship medal with Celtic in 1919, the same year he starred in an unofficial Victory International against Ireland. A further League title (1922) and Scottish Cup success (1923) followed before he departed Paradise. He was selected for Scotland's 1–0 win over England at Villa Park in 1922, which was the first victory on English soil since 1903 and gave the Scots the Home Championship. The following year he captained his country in a 2–2 draw with the Auld Enemy at Hampden. Willie won 5 full caps in total and also represented the Scottish League 4 times.

At the end of September 1923, when Celtic players were disappointed with the bonus system, Cringan acted as spokesman on their behalf and went to the directors with his team-mates' request for a wage increase. Within a month he was transferred to Third Lanark. He had a short spell with Motherwell before retiring in 1925 to play his other favourite sport of quoits, at which he became Scottish Champion in 1926.

His brother Jim played for Birmingham City (1922–34) and appeared in the 1931 FA Cup final, while his nephew Jimmy Davidson starred for Partick Thistle and Scotland in the 1950s.

# John Crum
### Forward 1932-1942

| | Appearances | Goals |
|---|---|---|
| League | 190 | 73 |
| Scottish Cup | 21 | 17 |
| Glasgow Cup | 13 | 8 |
| Charity Cup | 10 | 3 |
| Other Competitions | 86 | 41 |
| TOTAL | 320 | 142 |

The stars were certainly shining when this wonderful wee striker was born in Glasgow on New Year's Day 1912, for on that same afternoon a Jimmy Quinn hat-trick gave the Celts a 3–0 victory over old rivals Rangers at Parkhead.

A pawky 'gallus' Glaswegian raised in the north-west district of Maryhill, 'John's ability was first spotted by the famous junior outfit, Ashfield, and after making a name for himself leading their attack, he exchanged their black and white hoops for the green and white of Celtic in 1932.'

He graduated from the Bhoys' superb reserve side and despite his small stature (5ft 6in and 10st 4lb) could outjump much bigger opponents. He proved to be an extremely brave and nippy forward, always pressurising defences. A broken leg in 1934 barely dampened his enthusiasm and the cheerful little Celt recovered to hit the high spots at inside left. A man with relations from Derry, Crum won the first of two international caps for Scotland as outside right against England at Wembley on 4 April 1936, and gained the famous penalty equaliser by Tommy Walker after being clattered by Eddie Hapgood. He earned the deserved reputation of being a shrewd player off the ball with his uncanny positional sense and intelligent running; and as centre forward Johnny also played behind the attack (long before the 'Revie Plan') to develop a bewildering interchanging act that included himself Malcolm MacDonald and John Divers.

This terrific triangle had a telepathic understanding and were responsible for winning the League Championship and the Empire Exhibition Trophy in 1938. Crum's contribution to winning the latter was immense. He netted Celts' equaliser against Sunderland in round one; scored the only goal of the semi-final with Hearts; and, in the final against Everton he beat Ted Sager during the extra-time period 'then ran behind the goal to do a jig of joy for the Celtic end.' The previous year he had opened the scoring against Aberdeen in the Scottish Cup final in front of an incredible crowd of 146,433 at Hampden, and had won his first League Championship medal in 1936. Crum loved to play the piano, and fellow forward Malky MacDonald remembered him as a fly wee man who was great at dragging centre halfs out of the middle to leave space for others to run into. Another team-mate, Jimmy Delaney, recalled: 'What a bloke was wee Johnny.

Johnny Crum.

He was always joking. I remember one day the newspapers reported Sunderland had bid £22,000 for the pair of us. That morning at training, Johnny gave me his view of the bid. He said £20,000 had been bid for him and £2,000 for me. I answered by explaining to him that the full £22,000 had been bid for me and that he was being thrown in as an extra... just like a free gift.'

Crum had been studying to be a teacher when Hitler put paid to his ambition and he spent the war years working in the shipyards, where, for a change, he found himself on the same side as Rangers' rampaging centre forward Jimmy Smith.

He was surprisingly allowed to leave Paradise for Morton in 1942, and played with the Cappielow club for a few seasons until injury brought about his premature retirement from the game. After the war, Johnny worked as a salesman for a well-known Glasgow sports shop. This great Celt of the 1930s also represented the Scottish League and Scotland at junior level. He died in July 1969, aged fifty-seven.

# Kenny Dalglish
Forward 1967-1977

| | Appearances | Goals |
|---|---|---|
| League | 200 (4) | 112 |
| Scottish Cup | 30 | 11 |
| League Cup | 56 (3) | 35 |
| Europe | 27 (1) | 9 |
| Other Competitions | 16 (1) | 9 |
| TOTAL | 329 (9) | 176 |

When asked what Dalglish's best position was Jock Stein replied: 'With a player like Kenny you don't talk about positions; you just give him a jersey.'

Words alone cannot portray the vision of Kenny Dalglish shielding the ball, waiting for the precise moment to pass or make a quick turn into space to create a shooting opportunity. He was originally a goalkeeper with his primary school team, Milton Bank, and assistant-manager Sean Fallon tells how he came to Celtic in 1967, after having played for Possil YM and Glasgow United. 'Vic Davidson's mother recommended her son and Kenny Dalglish, who played in the same team. I signed Vic, no bother, but Kenny was a Rangers fan. On our wedding anniversary, on 4 May, we were on our way to Largs for a meal. Kenny lived in the flats overlooking Rangers' training ground. I told my wife I'd only be a minute. I went in to discover he'd just had a row with his father. It took me two hours to break the ice and persuade him to sign. Meanwhile my wife and girls were roasting in the car outside.'

Dalglish proved a highly skilful striker, razor sharp in his opponents' goal area. Unselfish and disciplined, he could read a game perfectly. Tommy Docherty once said: 'People say he lacks a yard in pace, but I say to them that he's ten yards quicker upstairs.' He scored over 100 League goals for Celtic and won four Championship medals, four Scottish Cup winners and a League Cup badge in the 1974/75 season. As skipper of the 1977 Scottish Cup final victory over Rangers, Kenny lost his medal at the end of the game. 'Police found it in the umbrella of a man in an invalid chair whom he had gone to greet.'

In August 1977 Dalglish cost Liverpool £440,000, then a record fee between British clubs. He spent many memorable seasons at Anfield, winning a host of honours, including three European Cup winner's medals – Kenny scored the winner in the 1978 Final at Wembley against FC Brugge. Voted the FWA Footballer of the Year in 1979, another century of goals saw him become the first player to score 100 in both the Scottish and English Leagues, and he is also the only man to collect all three domestic winner's medals on both sides of the border.

'King Kenny' represented Scotland at every level: schoolboy, youth, under-23 and full international, receiving a record 102 caps. He is Scotland's joint top scorer with 30 goals.

In June 1985, Dalglish became Liverpool's first player-manager, guiding them to the

A young Kenny Dalglish nets from the penalty spot against Rangers at Ibrox in August 1971.

League and Cup double in his first season in charge – a remarkable feat that neither Shankly nor Paisley achieved. The pressures, though, were intense and in February 1991 he surprised everyone by announcing his retirement from football after taking the Reds to three League titles and two FA Cup wins.

Suitably refreshed, he returned as manager of Blackburn Rovers, whom he led to promotion into the new Premiership via the play-offs in 1992. In 1995 he became only the third manager (after Herbert Chapman and Brian Clough) to win the top division with two different clubs. He had a brief time as boss at Newcastle United and in 1998 came within 90 minutes of the Tynesiders' first major domestic trophy in forty-three years. Even in his short spell in charge at Celtic in 2000 he won a trophy – the League Cup.

Awarded the MBE in 1984, and made a Freeman of Glasgow the following year, Kenny Dalglish – the master footballer, the master manager – doesn't have to prove himself to anyone. Quite simply he's done and won it all.

# Dixie Deans
Striker 1971-1976

| | Appearances | Goals |
|---|---|---|
| League | 122 (4) | 89 |
| Scottish Cup | 21 | 18 |
| League Cup | 21 (1) | 11 |
| Europe | 11 (3) | 6 |
| Other Competitions | 3 (1) | 1 |
| TOTAL | 178 (9) | 125 |

Not surprisingly nicknamed after the pre-war Everton and England centre forward Dixie Dean, John Kelly Deans made an immediate impact with Celtic after signing from Motherwell at the end of October 1971, for a bargain £17,500. He scored on his debut in a 5–1 thrashing of Partick Thistle at Firhill on 27 November 1971, and even when he missed a spot-kick in the European Cup semi-final penalty shoot-out against Inter Milan, Dixie redeemed himself a few weeks later by scoring only the second straight hat-trick in Scottish Cup final history in Celts' 6–1 hammering of Hibernian at Hampden.

Deans joined Motherwell in the autumn of 1965 and came to Parkhead with something of a reputation for indiscipline; indeed, he had got his marching orders at Celtic Park on 10 December 1966. Ordered off several times, Dixie at one stage threatened to end his career and emigrate. The breaking point came after being shown the red card against Stoke City in the Texaco Cup – he tabled a transfer request and the Motherwell directors agreed to let him go if a suitable offer was received.

Jock Stein channelled this chunky wee striker's untapped energies into prolific goalscoring. He hit the target an incredible six times in a 7–0 home win over Partick Thistle on 17 November

1973, and became the only man in Scottish football history to net a hat-tick in both domestic trophy finals when Celtic defeated Hibs 6–3 to lift the 1974/75 League Cup.

Despite his height (5ft 7in), Dixie could easily outjump taller opponents, and proved a real live wire in and around the penalty box. A Linwood lad, he began his career with Neilston Juniors, and won two full caps for Scotland against East Germany and Spain during the 1974/75 season. He transferred to Luton Town for £20,000 in the summer of 1976, before going on loan to Carlisle United and then to Partick Thistle on trial. He subsequently had three successful seasons in Australia with Adelaide City (formerly Juventus) and won the Philips Cup in 1979.

Dixie now lives in Baillieston where he runs a public house.

| | Appearances | Goals |
|---|---|---|
| League | 143 | 69 |
| Scottish Cup | 17 | 5 |
| Glasgow Cup | 12 | 2 |
| Charity Cup | 6 | 4 |
| Other Competitions | 168 | 98 |
| TOTAL | 346 | 178 |

Dazzling Delaney, wing wizard and hero to a generation of Celtic supporters, joined the club on provisional forms in September 1933 and permanently in August 1934 from Stoneyburn Juniors. An inspiring footballer of electric pace, Delaney was a dangerous raider on the break and scored many vital goals; although injury-prone he was nonetheless a brave forward. Rangers' great skipper Jock 'Tiger' Shaw once said: 'I doubt if there was ever a sportsman like Jimmy. He was the cleanest player I ever opposed. When you took the ball away from him, you did it with the knowledge that you wouldn't be tripped or pushed. I could have played against Delaney in my bare feet – and finished the game without a scratch, so fair was Jimmy in the tackle.'

He netted both Scotland's goals in a 2–0 win over Nazi Germany at Ibrox on 14 October 1936, and played in thirteen official peacetime internationals altogether, but Jimmy is perhaps best remembered for his last-minute winner in the 1946 Scotland v. England Victory fixture at Hampden Park.

A superb Delaney hat-trick beat Rangers 4–2 in the Charity Cup final of 1936, and he got a Scottish Cup winner's medal in 1937 sandwiched between League Championship badges in 1936 and 1938. Then came the injury which almost ended his career against Arbroath at Parkhead on 1st April 1939, when he suffered a horrendous arm fracture; indeed, so badly shattered was the limb that the surgeon considered amputation.

Delaney did well to recover and moved to Manchester United in February 1946 for £4,000. At Old Trafford he collected an FA Cup winner's medal in 1948 before being transferred to Aberdeen for £3,500 in November 1950. He signed for Falkirk in December 1951, then in January 1954 cost Derry City what was then an Irish League record fee of £1,500. That same year, Jimmy became the first man to win cup winner's medals in Scotland, England and Northern Ireland. In 1956 Cork Athletic threw away a two-goal lead to lose to Shamrock Rovers in the Republic's final, thus depriving Delaney, then in his forty-second year, what would have been a unique and surely unrepeatable feat.

Jimmy ended his career with Elgin City in the Highland League, and died in his native Cleland on 26 September 1989, aged seventy-five.

# Joe Dodds

Left-back 1908-1920, 1921-1922,

| | Appearances | Goals |
|---|---|---|
| League | 352 | 26 |
| Scottish Cup | 33 | 2 |
| Glasgow Cup | 16 | 1 |
| Charity Cup | 25 | 2 |
| Other Competitions | 7 | 0 |
| TOTAL | 433 | 31 |

'Need I say more about Dodds than that when he was playing in front of me, I never once had to come out for a cross-ball.' This was the amazing claim and praiseworthy tribute to the defensive qualities of Dodds by the legendary Scottish international goalkeeper Jimmy Brownlie.

Born in the Lanarkshire town of Carluke in the summer of 1887, Joe Dodds played for the local Milton Rovers side before entering Paradise in May 1908. A fierce competitor, he was always steady, and popular with the fans for his honest, hardworking style. Dodds was recorded as having a good turn of speed and being a clean and powerful kicker. He originally had considerable runs at centre and left-half with Celtic, and it wasn't until Jimmy Hay departed for Newcastle that he made the left-back berth his own, forming alongside Shaw and McNair arguably the safest defensive triangle in football.

Dodds starred in all three of Scotland's 1914 home international fixtures, including their emphatic 3–1 victory over England at Hampden Park. During the First World War he served in the Royal Field Artillery, then was loaned to the newly formed Dumfries club, Queen of the South, before moving to Cowdenbeath in the Central League for more money in 1920. In 1921 Celtic promised to give him a benefit, so he returned to the fold at Parkhead where his renewed understanding with Shaw and McNair led the Celts to Championship glory in the 1921/22 season. The directors reneged on their promise, so he left the club again and went back to Queen's Palmerston Park, where he assisted the Doonhamers for several seasons before retiring from the game.

Joe Dodds won eight Championship and three Scottish Cup winner's medals with Celtic and made eight appearances for the Scottish League, as well as playing in the annual Glasgow v. Sheffield match in 1913. He became reserves team trainer at Parkhead in the late 1930s and died on 14 October 1965, aged seventy-eight.

# Dan Doyle
Left-back 1891-1899

|  | Appearances | Goals |
|---|---|---|
| League | 113 | 4 |
| Scottish Cup | 21 | 2 |
| Glasgow Cup | 31 | 2 |
| Charity Cup | 11 | 0 |
| Other Competitions | 17 | 0 |
| TOTAL | 193 | 8 |

An early Celtic celebrity and the greatest full-back of his time, Dan Doyle starred for Scotland on eight occasions, five of them against England. His brash and bold personality was such that when he disappeared before the England *v.* Scotland international at Liverpool in 1895, the selectors, who had decided to replace him with Foyers, dared not break the news on his late return and quickly and quietly reinstated the redoubtable Dan. It says a lot for his play that he was chosen to captain Scotland twice more against England.

Born in Paisley on 16 September 1864, this powerfully built, curly-haired giant was a handsome and humorous all-round athlete, who made his Hibernian debut at Airdrie

in aid of striking Lanarkshire coalminers on 19 March 1887. He subsequently had spells with East Stirlingshire, Newcastle East End, Grimsby Town and Bolton Wanderers before teaming up with Scotland's long-jump champion Andrew Hannah at Everton in 1889.

When Celtic started bucking the English trend of draining the Scottish game of its talent in August 1891 by poaching Doyle and Alec Brady from Everton, the Football League temporarily boycotted the Glasgow club. It certainly proved an extremely adventurous move by the 'amateur' Celts. Meanwhile Everton made strenuous efforts to recover Doyle, including a High Court case for breach of contract, and were confident that their offer of £5 a week and the managership of a public house in Liverpool would lure him south again. To their surprise, Dan turned down the terms, being satisfied with his life in Glasgow as an 'amateur' and comfortable as the owner of a pub. Indeed, it was said that Doyle had 'asked for the Mersey Docks' as his share in any transfer back to Liverpool.

Dan Doyle inevitably became one of Celtic's most famous and popular players. He was also a full-back with a somewhat primitive method of dealing with flying wingers. English speed merchants found themselves shouldered over the touch-line before they could bring their sprinting powers into action.

Dan Doyle was left-back for this great Celtic side of the 1890s.

Away from football he charmed everyone, as the following tale conveys. Celtic were down in London for a match in the 1890s and were spending the night before the game at one of the capital's foremost hotels. Dan was observed descending the gilted staircase wearing an unusually well-tailored navy-blue suit. He took a seat amongst a group of football officials, helped himself to a cigar, pulled up a trouser leg and crossed his knees in an elegant gesture. He was seen to be wearing a dazzling rainbow-coloured sock. In the select company which frequented this fashionable hotel, such vulgarity in dress was scorned by most, but it also aroused the curiosity of a few. Soon, a small crowd gathered around Dan as he sat back in the chair, contentedly sucking his cigar. From the surrounding group began to come a series of remarks about his multi-coloured sock. Eventually Dan said, 'Bet you £5 you can't get its neighbour in London.'

'Right, Jock,' said an onlooker, a typical man-about-town ready to make a mug of this Scots joker. 'Make it a tenner.' 'Done!' said Dan. 'Lift up the other trouser leg then,' said the Londoner. Dan did so, to display a fine black cashmere sock. There was great laughter from the group, all enjoying the joke except, of course, for the humbled local who paid his bet and slunk off into the night.

A member of Celts' famous three Cup-winning team of 1891/92, 'Doyle adorned any game he took up; an expert billiards player, a splendid batsman, a great quoiter, an international bowler, the greatest left-back of all time, a champion jumper, here was the C.B. Fry in professional life.' Dan Doyle – one of Celtic's truly great players and personalities – died on 8 April 1918, aged fifty-three, from a malignant disease after a lingering illness.

# Johnny Doyle
Winger 1976-1981

|  | Appearances | Goals |
|---|---|---|
| League | 104 (14) | 15 |
| Scottish Cup | 16 (2) | 7 |
| League Cup | 29 (5) | 14 |
| Europe | 8 (3) | 1 |
| Other Competitions | 7 (2) | 2 |
| **TOTAL** | 164 (26) | 39 |

'A fan in a jersey' is an often over used phrase, but that is the best and most appropriate description of Johnny Doyle. Ironically it was an ordering off while playing for Ayr United against his beloved Celtic that brought about his boyhood dream of signing for the Hoops. He had been suspended by the SFA as a result of this misdemeanour, and immediately afterwards told a reporter in an interview, 'I'm fed up being kicked about for £30 a week, I want to go to Celtic.' One week later, on 15 March 1976, he signed for a club record fee of £90,000 just before the squad flew out to Germany for a European Cup Winners' Cup tie against the wonderfully named Sachsenring Zwickau.

Doyle began his playing career with Viewpark Boys' Guild before going to Somerset Park during the closed season of 1970. With tremendous acceleration and a fierce competitive spirit he soon established himself with the 'Honest Men' and received this appraisal of his attributes in 1973: 'Undoubtedly the fastest right winger in Scotland. Has the speed of a gazelle and with a real skill in dribbling, ball control and crossing.' Under-23 appearances and a full cap against Romania at Hampden followed in December 1975 (he was Ayr's first internationalist since Bob Hepburn in 1931).

After overcoming an injury on his Celtic debut at Dundee on 20 March 1976, he soon established a rapport with the Jungle to become a favourite of the supporters. Some of the club's most memorable moments were the work of the inimitable JD, such as his superb solo goal against St Mirren at a jam-packed Love Street in the Scottish Cup in 1980, when he gathered the ball deep in his own half and sliced through the Saints like a runaway train to net from an impossible angle. Only a fortnight later Paradise erupted after he squeezed between two defenders to bullet home an amazing header to put Celts 2–0 up on Real Madrid in the European Cup quarter-final first leg.

Although an inconsistent performer, when on song Johnny Doyle could destroy the most resolute of defences. Sadly he died from electrocution, aged only thirty, whilst working in the loft of his new home in Kilmarnock on 19 October 1981.

# Bobby Evans
Right-half 1944-1960

| | Appearances | Goals |
|---|---|---|
| League | 385 | 10 |
| Scottish Cup | 64 | 0 |
| League Cup | 88 | 1 |
| Glasgow Cup | 32 | 0 |
| Charity Cup | 23 | 0 |
| Other Competitions | 27 | 2 |
| TOTAL | 619 | 13 |

Red-haired Bobby Evans joined Celtic from St Anthony's in 1944 and, as a relentless tackler and masterful distributor of the ball, he became a firm favourite with the fans.

Glasgow-born Evans attended Pollokshaws secondary school and played for Sir John Stirling Maxwell Thistle Juveniles and Thornliebank Methodist before joining the Ants. Bobby later recalled how he learned of Celtic's interest during a Junior Cup semi-final at Firhill: 'I felt I was playing a good game and was really enjoying it – at least until the whistle went for half-time and we trooped into the pavilion. The secretary, Mr McGrogan, told me that Celtic were watching me. I was on toast for the whole of the second half and feel sure that, had I been told before the game, I probably would never have been allowed to sign for the Celts. Mr McGrogan probably thought that he was doing the right thing by me, but I wish to differ. However, before much time elapsed, I signed for Celtic.' An apprentice joiner, Evans made his debut as an inside forward in an unofficial wartime fixture against Albion Rovers on 19 August 1944, and it wasn't until the last League game of 1947/48 at Dens Park, with Celtic facing possible relegation, that he switched to right-half and remained there for well over a decade.

On 23 October 1948, he made his full international debut, replacing Billy Campbell, in a 3–1 win over Wales. It was the first of 48 full caps, only five fewer than George Young's then record, and they were equally divided between wing-half and centre half. Indeed, he played at centre half for Scotland before he did so for Celtic, taking over from the injured 'Corky' Young in Vienna and Budapest in 1955 and performing quite magnificently. Bobby also captained his country, leading them out twice against England. On the field Evans was a model of discipline and, if he proved rather sensitive to criticism off the pitch, he enjoyed a distinguished career at Parkhead and skippered the side to a League Cup final triumph over Partick Thistle in the 1956/57 season.

Skipper Bobby Evans holds aloft the League Cup after a replay win over Partick Thistle in season 1956/57.

He won a League Championship badge in 1954 and played in four Scottish Cup finals (two as a winner) and two winning League Cup teams. In the 1953 Coronation Cup, against the top clubs in Britain, he was in a class of his own. Deputy goalkeeper for club and country, although of medium height, Evans was extremely good in the air and his enthusiasm for the game remained undiminished even after being handicapped by a back injury in 1958.

Unfortunately, Bobby Evans left Paradise in May 1960 under a cloud, surrounded by rancour and bad publicity. He moved to Chelsea for a reported fee of £12,500, but the move was not a success. Evans was now thirty-three

and had lost his edge, so the young players emerging in Chelsea's team never fully felt the benefit of his experience. In May 1961 Bobby was appointed player-manager of Newport County, before moving to Morton in July 1962. He subsequently played for Third Lanark, and also acted as their trainer-coach from the close season of 1963 and player-manager during the 1964/65 campaign. He was nicknamed 'Dai' by his team-mates because of his Welsh surname.

This Celtic legend ended his career as a player with Raith Rovers, retiring in 1968 just before his forty-first birthday. He died at Airdrie on 1 September 2001, aged seventy-four.

# Sean Fallon

Full-back, Centre forward 1950-1958

| | Appearances | Goals |
|---|---|---|
| League | 178 | 8 |
| Scottish Cup | 31 | 2 |
| League Cup | 47 | 3 |
| Glasgow Cup | 13 | 2 |
| Charity Cup | 4 | 0 |
| Other Competitions | 5 | 4 |
| TOTAL | 278 | 19 |

Nicknamed the 'Iron Man' for his solid performances, Sean Fallon had an unusual introduction to Celtic, when Joe McMenemy, son of the great 'Napoleon', saved Sean's sister Lily from drowning in Lough Gill while on holiday in Sligo. Joe and his friends were invited to the Fallon household and Joe sent him presents of Willie Maley's book *The Story of the Celtic* and a club jersey. Fallon realised his ambition to become a Celt on St Patrick's Day 1950, after he had played as a Glenavon full-back for the Irish League against League of Ireland in Dublin.

Sean Ryan's excellent book, *The Boys In Green*, uncovered this little chestnut regarding the time Fallon was chosen to play in Belfast against England in 1950. 'Fallon was an interesting character. As a boy, he had dreamed of playing for Celtic and yet when he was first offered terms by the legendary Jimmy McGrory he turned them down. He also took four years off his age, thinking that Celtic would not retain interest in him if they knew he was twenty-six. "I had two passports – one for football and the real one", he said. He had never been selected for FAI but when news of his selection by the IFA broke, Cunningham sent him one of those famous letters, which in effect told him to pull out. "I was to get a cheque for £1,000 from Glenavon and a wrist watch in honour of the occasion", recalled

Fallon, "but as my father was in politics in Sligo and this was a very hot potato at the time, I very reluctantly pulled out. I was the last player from the Republic selected by the IFA and I felt I had let them down as I had said I would play." It was the end of an era. There would be no more all-Ireland teams. The split had been confirmed and the island would in future field two distinct teams in international competition, differing in this respect from most other sports.'

He was a mainstay of the side until a cartilage injury saw him accept medical advice and retire in 1958. Sean became Celts' assistant manager in 1965, and was given the freedom of his native County Sligo in 1967. Fallon took over as manager in a caretaker capacity for the 1975/76 campaign, when Jock Stein was absent due to injuries sustained in a car crash. After a further two years in charge of youth development he left Parkhead in 1978. He later became a director of Dumbarton and Clyde.

| | Appearances | Goals |
|---|---|---|
| League | 219 | 55 |
| Scottish Cup | 39 | 10 |
| League Cup | 59 | 11 |
| Glasgow Cup | 17 | 4 |
| Charity Cup | 17 | 4 |
| Other Competitions | 2 | 0 |
| TOTAL | 353 | 84 |

Fife-born Willie Fernie was a masterly and mesmeric dribbler, even though he often took this skill to extremes. 'Never pass the ball unless it is to your team's advantage,' advised Dan Murphy, the scout responsible for bringing the player to Parkhead. They were words that Willie would never forget.

Fernie began his career with Leslie Hearts and played in the 1948 Scottish Juvenile Cup final at Easter Road before signing for Celtic the following season and being farmed out to the local side Kinglassie Colliery. He eventually established himself in the inside right position, where he showed that beautiful silky touch. He occasionally appeared as a winger and latterly moved to right-half. He had a tremendous Coronation Cup campaign in 1953 and after the final victory over Hibernian, Charlie Tully noted: 'If Willie had a left foot, we'd have won the game at half-time!' Fernie was also the most influential figure on the field when Celtic

enjoyed a 7–1 thrashing of Rangers in the 1957/58 League Cup final.

The following year he was transferred to Middlesbrough for £17,500, where he came into contact with a young centre forward called Brian Clough. At no time did the two players see eye to eye: Clough's abrasiveness and Fernie's independent streak saw many angry exchanges. Yet in later years, Clough admitted that he would have done better to heed much of Fernie's advice.

After only a couple of seasons at Ayresome, Willie returned to Paradise for a reported £12,000. He scored in his last match against Rangers at Ibrox in September 1961, before moving to St Mirren for £4,000, where he gained a second successive Scottish Cup runners-up medal in 1962. Willie Fernie won all the domestic honours with Celtic, was capped twelve times by Scotland and made four appearances for the Scottish League.

After spells at Alloa and in Ireland with Bangor, he subsequently returned to Parkhead as youth coach and managed Kilmarnock from October 1973 to October 1977. Today, he runs a small taxi-cab business in the Castlemilk district of Glasgow.

# Patsy Gallagher
Inside right 1911-1926

| | Appearances | Goals |
|---|---|---|
| League | 432 | 187 |
| Scottish Cup | 32 | 9 |
| Glasgow Cup | 29 | 5 |
| Charity Cup | 25 | 7 |
| Other Competitions | 8 | 2 |
| TOTAL | 526 | 210 |

Patsy Gallagher is the one Celt who, even today, is instantly identifiable by his first name alone. Born in County Donegal on 16 March 1891, Patsy came to Scotland with his family when still a child and played for the juvenile sides Renfrew St James' and Clydebank Juniors before joining Celtic in the autumn of 1911. He was a tiny inside forward – fragile and slightly hunchbacked – who rarely weighed more than 8st, but his stamina, courage and skill more than compensated for that seemingly meagre build. Indeed, such a combination of skill, hardness and confidence gave his team-mates inspiration and left the fans on the terraces with a deep feeling of admiration and affection towards the wee man they rightly nicknamed the 'Mighty Atom'.

The legendary Hibernian and Scotland goalkeeper Willie Harper regarded Patsy as the best footballer he ever played against: 'I remember one time at Easter Road, we were leading 1–0 at half-time. Celtic were downhill in the second half. The ball was centred, Patsy got it, ran right through the Hibs team, side stepped me and scored. Then he took the ball out of the net and gave it to me.'

Being naturally fit, he was never troubled by weight problems and knew how to keep in shape. He had an acrobatic agility which bewildered defences as Rangers' wing wizard, Alan Morton, underlined in an interview shortly after Patsy's death in 1953, by paying him the following tribute: 'Our fellows used to say after one of those Old Firm games, "There's Patsy, off Scot-free and we're sore all over." In summing up a position and in taking the responsibility for getting a goal himself Patsy was absolutely unsurpassed in my time... There was never a player like him and I often wonder if we shall see his like again. I wish we could, just to show the present day players that we of Patsy Gallagher's time had something to boast about.'

Amongst those thousands who flocked to catch a glimpse of his dazzling dribbling skills were two young boys who would later be immortalised themselves as members of that wonderful side, the 'Wembley Wizards' – Alex James and Hughie Gallacher watched in amazement at Patsy's wriggling stop-go style and, indeed, James was so mesmerised by his magical ability that he named one of his children after Patsy. Gallagher certainly knew his worth and once refused to play for Ireland against England unless he got paid the large fee he demanded.

He served an apprenticeship in John Brown's shipbuilding yard at Clydebank during the First World War, and on being allowed to leave Celtic for Falkirk in October 1926 for £1,500,

The *Scottish Daily Express* cartoon strip of Patsy's famous equalising goal in the 1925 Scottish Cup final against Dundee.

he proved an influential and inspirational figure for the Bairns in knocking Rangers out of the 1927 Scottish Cup. Jimmy McGrory relates the following charming tale: 'There once was the very famous occasion when he dressed up as a woman to get out of the hotel at Dunbar when we were away for special training. He borrowed clothes from a woman worker in the hotel and lowered his own clothes in a bundle out of the bedroom window on to the lawn. Mr Maley was in the reception hall that night and Patsy, with a black veil over his face wasn't just content to slip out past the boss. He couldn't resist giving a high-pitched good-night to which he got a very courteous reply. Then off he went on the town after changing into his own clothes in a garden shed to the rear of the hotel. But his plan did not work 100 per cent. Mr Maley found out about it the next day and gave Patsy a real roasting.

I asked Patsy later on how the boss had found out but he would only reply: "It's a secret." Patsy received a benefit game on 4 January 1932, when a Celtic/Falkirk Select defeated a Scottish League XI 10–7 with Willie Hughes of Celtic scoring eight!

After retirement he was the landlord of the International Bar in Kilbowie Road, Clydebank, and became a ceaseless worker for charity. The 'Mighty Atom' died, after a long illness, at his home in Scotstoun on 17 June 1953, aged sixty-two. His sons Willie and Tommy played for Celtic and Dundee respectively, while one grandson Stuart played for Airdrie in the mid-1970s, and another, Kevin, more recently starred for Dundee United, Coventry City, Blackburn Rovers, Newcastle and Scotland.

# Chic Geatons
Wing-half 1928-1941

| | Appearances | Goals |
|---|---|---|
| League | 285 | 12 |
| Scottish Cup | 33 | 0 |
| Glasgow Cup | 20 | 2 |
| Charity Cup | 17 | 0 |
| Other Competitions | 36 | 2 |
| TOTAL | 391 | 16 |

A member of two great Celtic sides – 1931 Scottish Cup winners and 1938 League Champions and Empire Exhibition Trophy winners – Charles 'Chic' Geatons always gave good solid performances and played for the jersey. Born in Lochgelly, Fifeshire, he first starred for the local club of that name before coming to Parkhead during the 1927/28 season, making his Celtic debut on 24 September 1928 in a drawn Glasgow Cup semi-final against Third Lanark.

A physically powerful footballer, Geatons proved himself an able stalwart and soon became a regular fixture in the team's line-up, with some rough edges to his game early in his career being sufficiently knocked off over the years. Chic never collected a full international cap, but was nonetheless one of Scotland's finest half-backs and represented the Scottish League on five occasions. Geatons developed into a versatile performer and he was the man who took over from John Thomson in goal on that fateful afternoon at Ibrox in September 1931.

On 5 March 1938, while playing for the reserves at Shawfield, Chic feigned injury when he heard Celtic were losing 0–2 to Kilmarnock in the Scottish Cup, to get over to Parkhead and congratulate friend and former team-mate Jimmy McGrory on his new-found success. Chic regained his first team spot for the rest of the season as Celts raced to the League title, Charity Cup and Empire Exhibition Trophy triumphs.

He retired from playing just after the start of the Second World War, making his last appearance for Celtic in an unofficial wartime match at Boghead on 21 December 1940. Geatons became coach at Celtic Park on 8 October 1946, but his appointment lasted only four seasons before he resigned on 8 August 1950, in protest at the way the club was being run. Chic Geatons died in his home town on 20 June 1970. Celtic manager Jock Stein and old team-mates Jimmy McGrory and Matt Lynch attended the Requiem Mass and funeral in Lochgelly.

# Tommy Gemmell
Left-back 1961-1971

| | Appearances | Goals |
|---|---|---|
| League | 247 | 38 |
| Scottish Cup | 43 | 4 |
| League Cup | 74 | 10 |
| Europe | 51 | 11 |
| Other Competitions | 18 | 4 |
| TOTAL | 433 | 67 |

Glasgow born Tommy Gemmell was one of the first of a new breed, an attacking full-back who excited with his overlapping runs and powerful shooting at the dawn of an era which left behind defenders who were afraid to step over the halfway line. In addition, Gemmell used his venomous shot to great effect from direct free-kicks and penalties. He signed from Coltness United in July 1961 and got the nickname 'Danny Kaye' because of his resemblance to the American comedian. Tommy scored legendary goals in both the 1967 and 1970 European Cup finals, whilst his last-minute effort against Kilmarnock in 1969 brought Celtic a fourth successive League Championship.

Before the match in Lisbon, the well-known car dealer Ian Skelly and his father promised Tommy 30 gallons of petrol if he scored against Inter Milan. Weeks after the final, Gemmell went into one of Skelly's stations and, sure enough, there were 30 gallons of petrol waiting for him.

He made 18 full international appearances for Scotland, including a sending-off for retaliation in a World Cup qualifying game against West Germany which saw him dropped from the Celtic side due to meet St Johnstone in the 1969/70 League Cup final. Things were never the same in Paradise after that and, in December 1971, Gemmell joined Nottingham Forest for £40,000. He returned to Scotland with Dundee in July 1973, where he captained the club to a League Cup final victory over Celtic in his first season.

Tommy Gemmell retired at the end of the 1976/77 campaign to become Dundee's manager until April 1980. He later ran a hotel in Perthshire, and managed Albion Rovers. He now works for Sun Life Assurance. When Gemmell went to the City Ground, a young Martin O'Neill told Tommy that he loved his goal in the European Cup Final. Tommy replied: 'Which one?'

Now entertains the supporters as an after dinner speaker. He recently sold all his football medals at a Chirstie's Auction in Glasgow.

| | Appearances | Goals |
|---|---|---|
| League | 338 (26) | 15 |
| Scottish Cup | 34 (4) | 1 |
| League Cup | 40 (3) | 3 |
| Europe | 33 (1) | 0 |
| Other Competitions | 6 | 0 |
| TOTAL | 451 (34) | 19 |

Tigerish midfield competitor Peter Grant was noted for his ball-winning ability and great appetite for the game. Born in Bellshill on 30 August 1965, Grant came through the ranks of Celtic Boys' Club to make his first-team debut against Rangers at Ibrox on 21 April 1984, and accumulated Scottish Schools, Youth, Under-21, 'B', and full international honours during his time with the club. Grant's strength and aggression in the tackle endeared him to the Parkhead faithful, who nicknamed him 'Mad Dog', as a result of his determination and commitment to the Celtic cause.

He made his first appearance in a full international for Scotland when he came on as a substitute in the Rous Cup defeat at the hands of England at Hampden Park on 27 May 1989, notable for being the last annual fixture between the rival countries. Grant's adaptability allowed him to perform at both right-back and as sweeper, and his role as anchorman in midfield became crucial to the side when Roy Aitken departed to Newcastle United in January 1990.

A model professional and Celtic shareholder, Grant was also sarcastically dubbed 'Peter the Pointer' by the supporters because of his traffic warden antics in ordering team-mates to guard opponents. In the 1995 Scottish Cup final victory over Airdrieonians, he performed magnificently and thoroughly deserved his Man of the Match award.

Peter signed for Norwich City on 22 August 1997 for £200,000, and his vast experience helped bring along the Canaries' youthful side. In recent years he completed the SFA's advanced coaching course at Largs, and after a stint as assistant-manager of AFC Bournemouth is now assistant at West Ham United.

| | Appearances | Goals |
|---|---|---|
| League | 4 | 3 |
| Scottish Cup | 13 | 14 |
| Glasgow Cup | 7 | 4 |
| Charity Cup | 2 | 1 |
| Other Competitions | 10 | 8* |
| TOTAL | 36 | 30* |

'Darling' Willie Groves possessed striking good looks and mazy dribbling skills which dazzled opponents and delighted crowds everywhere. A Leith-born lad and protégé of Hibernian FC, Groves was a brilliant foraging forward with exquisite ball control and a fine flair for passing. In 1887, after three consecutive Scottish Cup semi-final appearances, his genius gave Hibs the impetus to win the national trophy for the first time, but only after surviving a protest for professionalism by his semi-final victims, Vale of Leven.

The youngster went west in 1888 and soon became the idol of the Celtic supporters. On one memorable occasion, he scored a spectacular winning goal in a Scottish Cup first-round home tie against Rangers; *Scottish Sport* caught the moment vividly for posterity: 'When Groves scored the goal, T. Maley, who was umpiring, waved his flag in jubilation. The Rangers players stared in blank amazement, the Celtic players shook hands effusively, the stands rose bareheaded to a man cheering vociferously, the crowds lining the railing did much the same thing, and the noise that little manoeuvre evoked could have been heard at Ibrox Park; it rose and swelled into one ground note of triumph that bore in its tone the delighted response of ten thousand thankful hearts.'

He endeavoured to go into the drinks business, only to be turned down by the licensing court. *Scottish Sport* alleged that Celtic had provided £500 for the Groves venture. Willie won an apology and damages estimated between £50 and a fiver, even though the accusation was probably true.

Groves soon tired of the Scottish attitude towards professional football and moved south to the Black Country club West Bromwich Albion in October 1890. After going to The Hawthorns, Groves dropped back to become an exceptional left-half. This move, prompted perhaps by the treatment meted out to him as a forward, was a success and the renowned half-back line of Reynolds, Perry and Groves provided the nucleus of West Brom's FA Cup triumph in 1892, Willie making two of the three goals that helped defeat Aston Villa. Ironically, the following year, Groves joined arch-rivals Villa and helped them begin their dominance of English soccer in the 1890s by winning the League Championship in the 1893/94 season. Sadly his health gave way in 1894 and he spent the summer at Bournemouth. Indeed, he was so seriously ill that he was unable to get in touch with the club, where a rumour had started that he had emigrated to America. This was patently false, but Willie never played again for the Birmingham outfit.

Celtic c. 1889. Groves is front row, right.

Meanwhile, Scotland had swept aside the cant and humbug by legitimising professional football. So in 1895, he returned to Edinburgh, a shadow of his former self, giving only glimpses of his awesome ability – a has-been at the age of twenty-six. Hibs took a gamble and played him in the 1896 Scottish Cup final against Hearts, but sadly the gamble failed and from Easter Road he went to the obscure Northamptonshire club, Rushden.

On returning to Midlothian, Groves drifted away from the game towards poverty and ill-health, suffering a heart condition. A week before his death, the Rosebery Charity Committee voted to raise a small sum for his benefit, but he died at Longmore Hospital on 14 February 1908. He was thirty-nine years old, a tragic end to a man described as a 'picturesque figure' in his playing days – a sort of Romeo in the sport with his raven locks and classic-cut features. Writers went into raptures over his masterful footwork: 'When he got the ball at his foot, forward went his head, up went his shoulders threading his way through a maze of opponents, feeling his way, for he worked by instinct and certainly not by sight.' A fitting tribute to a fabulous footballer.

# Frank Haffey
Goalkeeper 1958-1964

| | Appearances | Shut-outs |
|---|---|---|
| League | 139 | 41 |
| Scottish Cup | 34 | 10 |
| League Cup | 24 | 9 |
| Europe | 3 | 1 |
| Other Competitions | 17 | 1 |
| TOTAL | 217 | 62 |

Govan boy Frank Haffey began his career with Greenock Juveniles and signed for Campsie Black Watch at the beginning of the 1957/58 season. The Celtic scout Willie Cowan gave him a trial against Rangers Reserves at Ibrox on New Year's Day 1958, and the Second XI coach Jock Stein decided shortly after half-time that he would like to sign him. The following day he met manager McGrory and joined the club before being loaned out to Maryhill Harp.

He was a talented goalkeeper, although one perhaps prone to eccentric behaviour. It is unfortunate that Haffey, fine 'keeper though he was, is best remembered for conceding nine goals against England at Wembley in 1961. Later that day, at King's Cross station, cameramen cruelly photographed him under a sign which read 'Platform 9'. Only the previous year Haffey had saved a Bobby Charlton penalty kick as Scotland earned a creditable 1–1 draw against the Auld Enemy at Hampden, but then that was conveniently forgotten after the Wembley débâcle. Amongst Frank's other feats were a headed clearance whilst wearing a 'bunnet', a missed penalty against Airdrie and being one of the first players to record a song. Despite his flair for the unorthodox, he was often an extremely capable and most agile custodian, with his display in the replayed 1963 Scottish Cup final scarcely bettered by any Celtic goalie.

A broken ankle at Firhill effectively ended his career at Parkhead, and in October 1964 he turned down the chance to join Third Lanark and transferred to Swindon Town instead for £8,000. He subsequently emigrated to Australia, where he starred for a number of clubs including St George Budapest, Hakoah and Sutherland. On retirement he entertained in night clubs as a cabaret singer.

| | Appearances | Goals |
|---|---|---|
| League | 126 (3) | 6 |
| Scottish Cup | 29 | 1 |
| League Cup | 45 | 5 |
| Europe | 25 | 0 |
| Other Competitions | 9 | 0 |
| TOTAL | 234 (3) | 12 |

Utility man Davie Hay could fill almost any outfield position with consummate ease. 'A stern defender, effective ball-winner, strong shot and superb in distribution' sums up Hay's remarkable versatility. On the advice of a priest, Sean Fallon signed the sixteen-year-old St Mirin's Boys' Guild player during the 1964/65 season for the romantic price of two footballs.

Whether in defence or midfield, Hay always performed with a commendable competitive spirit. Indeed, Scotland manager Tommy Docherty nicknamed him 'The Quiet Assassin' in light of his unassuming attitude and fierce tackling. In the 1973/74 campaign, he had a number of disagreements with Celtic over trivial issues, did not turn up for training and found himself suspended by the club. Nevertheless, Hay had a magnificent 1974 World Cup finals in West Germany, being the inspiration of Scotland's unbeaten series of games. Shortly afterwards, in July 1974, he was transferred to recently relegated Chelsea for £225,000.

Playing his heart out in a poor Chelsea team, he lost his place in the Scotland side and later suffered serious injuries. At Stamford Bridge, Hay had five operations, including two on an eye, and ultimately had to retire in September 1979. He became Motherwell's assistant manager in November 1979, progressing to manager before taking charge at Celtic in July 1983.

Davie had a season as boss of St Mirren 1991/92, but with relegation from the Premier Division took up a coaching appointment in America as youth director of Tampa Bay Rowdies. In the summer of 1993 Davie became assistant to ex-Celt John Gorman at Swindon Town, but resigned the following year before being given the position of chief scout with Celtic by Tommy Burns. Like so many others he fell foul of Fergus McCann. He led Livingston to League Cup glory in 2004, but left soon after. Manager of Dunfermline Athletic in 2004/05, he resigned before the end of the season.

# James 'Dun' Hay

Left-back, Left-half 1903-1911

| | Appearances | Goals |
|---|---|---|
| League | 217 | 15 |
| Scottish Cup | 40 | 5 |
| Glasgow Cup | 30 | 1 |
| Charity Cup | 11 | 2 |
| Other Competitions | 19 | 0 |
| TOTAL | 317 | 23 |

Legendary left-half and captain of Celtic. Born in the small village of Woodside, near Annbank on 9 February 1881, James 'Dun' Hay was a powerful leader and became a sound, skilful and courageous skipper of the side which won six League Championships on the trot. He was better known to the vast band of Celtic supporters as the 'General' and 'The man with the iron chest'.

Hay won the first of eleven international caps on 18 March 1905, against Ireland at Parkhead, and according to his Scotland team-mate, the goalkeeper Jimmy Brownlie, Jimmy was a 'real personality man, broad-shouldered and deep-chested'. Brownlie continued: 'His strongest feature was his positional play. He had an uncanny sense of anticipation and was the strongest of tacklers. A great captain, he had the power to urge on a team to better things when the run of the game wasn't going too well. His striking figure simply oozed domination – and what a quiet, shy, fellow he was away from the field. He is my greatest left-half.'

Jimmy also made six appearances for the Scottish League and twice represented Glasgow against Sheffield during an illustrious career which saw him collect all the domestic honours available.

After a dispute with manager Willie Maley over terms, Hay joined Newcastle United in July 1911 for £1,250. He replaced the great Peter McWilliam and almost helped Newcastle to a League Championship in his first season at St James's Park. He returned north to Ayr United in the summer of 1915 and spent many seasons at Somerset. He later held the post of secretary-manager with both Clydebank (1923–24) and Ayr United (1924–January 1926).

Jimmy 'Dun' Hay viewed the game's rulers with some cynicism and his career in management ended in 1926, when he was suspended for accusing a director of the club of bribery. The suspension was lifted during the 1927/28 term, but Hay never came back into football and died in his native Ayrshire on 4 April 1940. Four surviving members of the great Celtic team of 1904-10 attended the funeral at Ayr Cemetery – Jimmy Quinn, Alec McNair, Joe Dodds and Willie Loney, Jimmy McGrory, by then the Kilmarnock manager, sent a wreath.

# Bobby Hogg
Right-back 1931-1948

| | Appearances | Goals |
|---|---|---|
| League | 278 | 0 |
| Scottish Cup | 34 | 0 |
| League Cup | 10 | 0 |
| Glasgow Cup | 18 | 1 |
| Charity Cup | 16 | 0 |
| Other Competitions | 259 | 0 |
| TOTAL | 615 | 1 |

At seventeen years old, Bobby Hogg became the youngest professional in the Scottish League when he signed for Celtic from Royal Albert in May 1931. As a strong, dependable defender, Hogg took over from Willie Cook (who had been transferred to Everton), and continued in the right-back berth until after the war, altogether making over 600 peace-time and wartime appearances for Celtic. He made his first and last outings in the Hoops at Hampden. His League debut was in a 4–1 defeat at the hands of amateurs Queen's Park on 17 September 1932 and he played his last game on 8 May 1948, in a 2–0 Charity Cup final defeat by Rangers. Defending with commendable steadiness, Hogg would frequently take the heat out of a situation with a sharp tackle and thoughtful clearance.

Forever a travelling reserve, his only official international cap was won in Prague against Czechoslovakia on 15 May 1937, Scotland winning comfortably 3–1. Bobby also made six Scottish League appearances and played once for Scotland in a wartime international against England, at Newcastle on 8 February 1941, when the Scots won 3–2. With Celtic he won two League Championship (1936, 1938) and two Scottish Cup winner's medals (1933, 1937).

In December 1948, in the twilight of his career, Hogg was transferred to Alloa and was briefly manager of that team. A magnificent club servant, Bobby's only goal for Celtic (in the Glasgow Cup on 25 August 1936) came from a fortuitous long punt downfield, which the Third Lanark goalkeeper lost in the glare of the sun. A motor mechanic by trade, he died in Paisley on 15 April 1975. He had been discharged from hospital just a few weeks earlier having undergone two major operations. His son, Bobby junior, was once on Hearts' books.

# Harry Hood

Forward 1969-1976

| | Appearances | Goals |
|---|---|---|
| League | 161 (29) | 74 |
| Scottish Cup | 25 (4) | 13 |
| League Cup | 53 (12) | 24 |
| Europe | 24 (6) | 12 |
| Other Competitions | 10 (4) | 3 |
| TOTAL | 273 (55) | 126 |

The versatile forward Harry Hood's presence on the pitch at Parkhead was often greeted by the 'Hare Krishna' chant. Born in Glasgow on 3 October 1944, he attended a school where rugby predominated, but nonetheless became a soccer prodigy with Brunswick Youth Club. Hood entered the senior game at Clyde before moving south to Sunderland in November 1964, for £30,000. Harry never settled on Wearside and after making 31 League appearances and scoring 9 goals, he returned to Shawfield two years later for a reported £13,000 fee.

Alas he did not represent Scotland at full international level, but played four times in the unofficial world summer tour of 1967 and scored against England in his only Under-23 game at Hampden on 7 February 1968.

Harry joined Celtic on 16 March 1969, for £40,000, and was selected for the Scottish League against the League of Ireland on 2 September 1970. He scored some crucial goals during the 1970/71 season: these included the all-important opener at Pittodrie on 17 April 1971 to stop Aberdeen taking the title, and Celts' winner in the Scottish Cup final replay a few weeks later. The same term also saw him finish as Scotland's leading marksman with 22 League goals. In 1973/74 he hit a hat-trick in the League Cup semi-final win over Rangers, and also netted in the convincing 3–0 Scottish Cup final victory against Dundee United.

Harry Hood served the Bhoys for seven successful seasons as an influential and multi-talented footballer, being both a brilliant passer of the ball and a regular marksman. A master of unexpected attacking moves, he won all the domestic honours while with Celtic.

Given a free transfer on 29 April 1976, he went to NASL side San Antonio Thunder at the beginning of May 1976, and became the US team's top scorer with 10 goals and 7 assists from twenty starts. After an unproductive term at Motherwell, he ended his playing career in Dumfries with Queen of the South. In the early 1980s he had brief periods in charge of Albion Rovers and Queen of the South. He now owns and runs the Angels Hotel in Uddingston.

# John Hughes
Centre forward, Outside left 1960-1971

|  | Appearances | Goals |
|---|---|---|
| League | 252 (3) | 116 |
| Scottish Cup | 50 (1) | 25 |
| League Cup | 68 (1) | 38 |
| Europe | 38 (2) | 10 |
| Other Competitions | 22 | 13 |
| TOTAL | 430 (7) | 202 |

Tall and quite weighty for a winger, John Hughes scored some spectacular goals, often the result of strong surges from deep positions, a ploy for which he became well known. Nicknamed 'Yogi' after the lovable cartoon character, 'Feed the bear' was the chant which roared from the Jungle enclosure as big John Hughes charged down the flank or through the middle on yet another rampaging run that left defenders floundering at his heels.

He joined Celtic from Shotts Bon Accord in 1960 and, although inconsistent, 'Yogi' nevertheless excited the Parkhead faithful throughout the 1960s with his electric pace, thunderous shots and powerful headers. It often seemed that for half a game he would keep running into opponents or falling over the ball like a man with two left feet. Then, suddenly, he would explode into some incredible feat of brilliance. A classic example was the day at Greenock in 1964, with Celts trailing 1–0 in a Scottish Cup tie. Just when it seemed he was to have 'one of those days', Hughes gathered the ball on the halfway line and waltzed past four defenders before unleashing an unstoppable shot into the top corner of the net from the edge of the penalty area. On another memorable afternoon

in 1965, Celtic demolished Aberdeen 8–0 on an icy pitch with 'Yogi', wearing white sandshoes, scoring an astonishing five goals.

When things went wrong, Hughes' style of play – eyes down and run – prompted one terracing wag to remark, 'Hughes, you're nothing but a bingo player!' When on song, his terrific turn of speed and nimble footwork would cause panic amongst even the best-organised defences. A famous full-back once said of Hughes: 'You think he has lost his balance, then suddenly, he is past you and you realise you should have been watching the ball and not John.'

Along with Willie Wallace he moved to Crystal Palace in October 1971, for £30,000. After a brief stint at Sunderland (where he teamed up with his brother Billy), he coached Baillieston Juniors; was manager of Stranraer in 1975/76 and also became the Scottish Junior FA's first national manager in September 1978. He now runs a public bar only a free kick from Celtic Park.

# Maurice Johnston

Striker 1984-1987

| | Appearances | Goals |
|---|---|---|
| **League** | 97 (2) | 52 |
| **Scottish Cup** | 14 | 6 |
| **League Cup** | 8 | 9 |
| **Europe** | 6 | 4 |
| **Other Competitions** | 1 (1) | 1 |
| **TOTAL** | 126 (3) | 72 |

Wee 'MoJo' proved to be a quicksilver striker with a superb smash-and-grab style who could time his jump to such perfection that goalkeepers often had barely reacted by the time the ball was flashing past them into the net. An apprentice cutter before making the grade with Partick Thistle in 1981, he had previously played for St Roch's secondary school, Eastercraigs, Leeds United BC and Milton Battlefield. Celtic's boss Davie Hay kept a watchful eye on him at Firhill, but signed Jim Melrose instead and Johnston departed to Watford in November 1983 for £200,000. He teamed up with John Barnes at Vicarage Road and scored 23 goals in only 37 League appearances, and it was that sort of form that saw him become the most expensive player in the Premier Division when Celtic brought him back to Scotland for £400,000 in October 1984. Mo made his home debut on 13 October,

against Hibernian, and he scored the very next week at Tannadice in a 3–1 win over Dundee United. He transferred in the summer of 1987 to French club Nantes for £373,600, a fee which would have been almost trebled had he decided to go to England.

He was something of a controversial figure. In May 1989 he was paraded in Paradise wearing a Celtic jersey, yet within two months he had signed for arch-rivals Rangers. The Ibrox club broke with its Protestant tradition by buying the Catholic Johnston for £1.5 million and the eight-week saga finally came to an end. Celtic's supporters felt let down, to say the least, but in Govan Johnston continued to do his usual competent professional job of scoring goals until being sold to Everton, for another £1.5 million fee, in November 1991.

Less than two years later he returned to Scotland on a free transfer when he signed for Hearts. However, at Tynecastle he failed to get on with the manager, Tommy McLean, and was offloaded to Falkirk in March 1995. Maurice Johnston has more recently captained Kansas City Wizards to the Major League Soccer Championship in the USA. Now assistant coach to New York/New Jersey Metro Stars.

| | Appearances | Goals |
|---|---|---|
| League | 298 (10) | 82 |
| Scottish Cup | 47 (1) | 11 |
| League Cup | 87 (5) | 21 |
| Europe | 63 (1) | 16 |
| Other Competitions | 17 (3) | 5 |
| TOTAL | 512 (20) | 135 |

Wing wizard Jimmy 'Jinky' Johnstone teased and tormented defences for over a decade in Scottish football. The youngest of five children, as a boy he modelled himself on Stanley Matthews and spent hours perfecting the dribbling skills that were to make him a household name. From being a Parkhead ballboy, Johnstone signed for the club in 1961 and went on to become an idol of the Celtic supporters. A mazy meandering style gained him the nickname of 'Jinky' – and after one inspired performance in a European Cup tie against Nantes, he was dubbed the 'Flying Flea' by the French press. It was a rather inappropriate title, for Jimmy had such a terrible fear of flying that in the summer of 1967, after the Alfredo di Stefano testimonial match in Madrid, he arranged to take a holiday in Spain with his family and the story goes that he hired a taxi to take them 400 miles – and charged it to the club!

In that same year of triumphs the wee man came third in the European Footballer of the Year Awards (the highest position ever for a Scottish-based player). However, he was never really given the chance to show his great talent at international level; his 23 caps were scant reward for an undoubted genius and said more about his brushes with authority than the quality of his rivals. He was rarely accepted by most of the Scotland support; Ian St John recently

recalled that the players had to pull off a so-called 'Scotland fan' from attacking Jimmy on the team bus after a game against Wales. Kevin Keegan selected him for his all-time British side, noting: 'Jimmy should have won 100 caps and not the two dozen or so he received', whilst Jock Stein felt his biggest achievement in football was being able to keep him in the game for five years more than might otherwise have been expected.

He left Parkhead in 1975 for the NASL side San José Earthquakes and later starred briefly with Sheffield United, Dundee, Shelbourne, Elgin City and Blantyre Celtic before retiring. Even then he wasn't finished. Charlie Nicholas recalled a five-a-side match 24 hours before the 'Old Firm' League Cup final of 1982/83: 'Wee Jimmy came along that day and joined in and we couldn't get the ball off him for 20 minutes. We all stopped and I was looking at Davie Provan and Frank McGarvey and Danny

Wing wizard Jimmy Johnstone takes on the Benfica defence at Parkhead in the European Cup in November 1969.

McGrain and thinking this isn't supposed to be happening because we're practising for a big game. He was there for 20 minutes with the ball, sitting on it, doing everything with it. I've never seen an exhibition like it. Unbelievable he was.' Subsequently a truck driver for Lafferty's, he had a spell coaching Celtic's S form signings under Davie Hay's charge in the mid-1980s.

The famous movie actor Robert Duval regards Johnstone as one of the best personalities he has ever met and named his dog 'Jinky' in his honour. Sadly, the wee man was diagnosed as having motor neurone disease in November 2001, but if anybody can fight such an illness, it's the player who used to bounce back to his feet everytime he was kicked to the ground. He was recently voted the club's all-time greatest player by the supporters.

# James Kelly
Centre half 1888-1897

| | Appearances | Goals |
|---|---|---|
| League | 106 | 9 |
| Scottish Cup | 35 | 2 |
| Glasgow Cup | 33 | 4 |
| Charity Cup | 17 | 2 |
| Other Competitions | 20 | 0* |
| TOTAL | 211 | 17 |

Born in the village of Renton, Dunbartonshire, on 15 October 1865, James Kelly served Celtic in one capacity or another from the club's first match until his death on 20 February 1932. Originally an outside right, he moved to centre half around 1887, while starring with the famous local club Renton, who at the time were the finest team in Britain. In fact he was a member of the Renton side which beat the English FA Cup winners, West Bromwich Albion, in the 'World Championship' match at Hampden Park in May 1888.

He was regarded as the most outstanding footballer in the country, and indeed Celts' first side was built around this heroic figure. A clean tackler and fine distributor of the ball, Kelly proved to be the perfect pivot – always very attack-minded, roving upfield whenever possible, hoping to create an opening, and renowned as an 'exploiter of long drop-shots'.

The club's first captain, he topped his two Scottish Cup medals at Renton by collecting three League Championship badges, a Scottish Cup and numerous Glasgow and Charity Cup medals with Celtic. He retired from the playing side of the game in 1897 to become a director

and was elected chairman of the board in 1909, a post he held until 1914.

Owner of three public houses, Kelly subsequently made his mark in life as a Lanarkshire county councillor and JP as well as serving on the Blantyre School Board for many years. He was arguably one of the finest pivots football had ever known, receiving eight Scotland international caps and also representing the Scottish League, Dumbartonshire and Glasgow Association. He was father of six footballing sons, one of whom – Robert – also became a Celtic director and ultimately chairman of the club.

| | Appearances | Shut-outs |
|---|---|---|
| League | 263 | 75 |
| Scottish Cup | 32 | 8 |
| Glasgow Cup | 16 | 3 |
| Charity Cup | 16 | 2 |
| Other Competitions | 5 | 3 |
| TOTAL | 332 | 91 |

The Canadian keeper James 'Joe' Kennaway was born in Montreal on 25 January 1905, one of four children. In October 1930 he set sail on the *Duchess of Richmond* from Montreal on a week's voyage to Liverpool, arriving on Merseyside on 30 October, and made a commendable Celtic debut the following day in a 2–2 draw at Motherwell. The *Sunday Post* headline read 'Kennaway Has Come To Stay' and reported: 'Kennaway's style of taking high shots took the breath away from one at times. He has, however, a very quick eye and movement. He appears to prefer a smart palm-away to a clutch and a spectacular clearance. Only twice had he to dive to a ball. Once he was lucky to see it pass the upright. On the other occasion he stopped its progress in the nick of

time.' He soon settled into his new surroundings and became the mainstay replacement for the late John Thomson.

Kennaway's goalkeeping prowess first attracted attention when he was playing for the old Montreal Canadian Pacific Railway team during the early 1920s, and he played for Canada in their 6–2 defeat by the USA in Brooklyn on 6 November 1926. Despite the result, he impressed the Americans and the next year signed for the Providence, Rhode Island, a club which played in the American Soccer League. In May 1931, after the entire Providence team transferred to Fall River, he performed heroics in goal against a touring Celtic side to record a 1–0 win for Fall River. Maley remembered this outstanding display against the hoops, invited him over and a deal was made through John F. Rooney. A firm favourite with the vast Celtic support, on match days at Parkhead a flamboyant fan in the stand known as 'Big Arthur' developed the ritual of shouting 'Hello there, Joe!' when he appeared on the pitch – this was the cue for Joe to wave back to him in response.

The sports journalist James Gordon recalled: 'In the 1933 Scottish Cup final against Motherwell, he made the best save I have ever seen. Scottish internationalist Willie McFadyen let go a shot from about 15 yards and Joe dived

'Keeper Kennaway punches clear the danger of Aberdeen raid during the 1937 Scottish Cup final.

and, while still going through the air, punched the ball which landed well outside the penalty area. As Celtic won by a margin of 1–0 you can see that it was a vital save.' When the final whistle sounded, Joe Kennaway became the first foreign player to gain a Scottish Cup winner's medal.

His inspired performances led to international recognition and he was first selected for Scotland against Wales on 4 October 1933. Alas, just before the team left for Cardiff, he went down with 'flu and was replaced by Jack Harkness, who went straight to Kennaway's house on his return to Glasgow and gave him his goalkeeping sweater with the Lion crest on it. Harkness said: 'I felt that it morally belonged to him.' However, he played for Scotland against Austria at Hampden less than two months later, and is thus the only man to have kept goal for two different countries. Kennaway possessed reliable reflexes and anticipation and was one of

the first custodians to throw a ball rather than kick it downfield. He performed consistently until the outbreak of the Second World War and was a regular fixture of Celts' successful side of the late 1930s.

The man who sparred with World Champion boxer Benny Lynch left Britain in 1940, returning to Montreal to work for Vickers and star for their soccer team. Joe Kennaway was without doubt the greatest goalkeeper Canada has ever produced and one of its finest sportsmen, yet on his untimely death on 7 March 1969, only the *Montreal Star* of his home-town newspapers mentioned his passing, and that in form of a simple death notice placed there by his family. Canadian soccer historian Colin Jose tried to have Kennaway inducted into the Canadian Sports Hall of Fame but they rejected his overtures, saying that they did not know what standard of football Celtic played!

# Paul Lambert

Midfielder 1997-2005

| | Appearances | Goals |
|---|---|---|
| League | 180 (12) | 14 |
| Scottish Cup | 19 (4) | 1 |
| League Cup | 10 (1) | 2 |
| Europe | 44 (3) | 2 |
| Other Competitions | 0 | 0 |
| TOTAL | 253 (20) | 19 |

Almost everything Celtic did on the football pitch passed through the master of midfield Paul Lambert, and I'm sure if anyone was to analyse the entire duration of a game, nine times out of ten Paul's possession of the ball would have far outweighed that of any other outfield player. A key cog not only in Celts' wonderful sides of 1997/98 and 2000/01, but also in Borussia Dortmund's European Cup-winning team of 1996/97, Paul Lambert was a world-class midfielder.

Born in Glasgow on 7 August 1969, he represented Scotland at under-15 schoolboy level and graduated to Paisley's Love Street from Linwood Rangers B. Making his St Mirren debut at the tender age of sixteen as a substitute in a 2–1 win over Motherwell at Fir Park on 16 April 1986. In 1987, whilst still only seventeen, he helped the Buddies to Scottish Cup glory with a 1-0 final victory over Dundee United at Hampden Park.

Alex Smith tried to take him to Aberdeen in 1989, but baulked at Saints' asking price of £750,000. Lambert then rejected a Jim McLean offer in 1992 before eventually signing for his brother Tommy at Motherwell on 7 September 1993. St Mirren were by then a cash-strapped First Division side and they let Paul go for a mere £100,000 plus Jim Gardiner. Turned down by Dick Advocaat at PSV Eindhoven, Lambert's European agent Ton van Dalen got him a trial and lucrative deal with Borussia Dortmund in 1996 under the Bosman ruling. At Dortmund he sat next to the future Rangers goalkeeper Stefan Klos on matchday coach journeys, and set up Borussia's opener for Karl-Heinz Riedle in their 3–1 European Cup final victory against Juventus at the Olympic Stadium, Munich, in 1997. The astute Wim Jansen felt Paul could do a job for Celtic, and with Lambert's wife unsettled and homesick, he finally got his man in November 1997 after an incredibly emotional send-off from Borussia's fans.

A crucial member of Scotland's 1998 World Cup squad, that same summer to his consternation he learned that workmen discovered an old wartime bomb underneath the pitch of Dortmund's Westfalen stadium. Bertie Vogts persuaded him to return, as captain, to the international set-up, before Lambert became manager of Livingston in May 2005.

# Henrik Larsson
Forward, 1997-2004

| | Appearances | Goals |
|---|---|---|
| League | 218 (3) | 174 |
| Scottish Cup | 25 | 23 |
| League Cup | 11 | 10 |
| Europe | 58 | 35 |
| Other Competitions | 0 | 0 |
| TOTAL | 312 (3) | 242 |

This phenomenal Swedish striker was born in Helsingborg on 20 September 1971. His popularity at Parkhead was such that when fans bought a Celtic jersey with a seven on the back they simply put GOD above the number instead of the player's name.

His father, Francisco Rocha, was a sailor from the Cape Verde islands, just off the west coast of Africa, but Henrik's parents decided to give him his mother's maiden name to underline his Swedish nationality. He first played for the schoolboy side Hogaborg, and this team today honours Henrik with the Henke-ball, which is an annual prize for the sixteen-year-old who performs the most consistently over the season.

In 1991 he joined Helsingborg for £300 a month without bonuses, and scored 34 goals in his first term as the club won promotion to the top division for the first time in twenty-two years. Larsson then moved into the big time in September 1993, with a transfer to Feyenoord of Holland for a £295,000 fee. Coach Wim Jansen had gone to Sweden to look at another striker who had been recommended to him. However, Henrik was the most impressive player on the pitch with his quick feet, high technical quality and good heading ability. Jansen forgot all about his initial target and signed the stylish Swede. Larsson scored with a header on his international debut for Sweden in a 3–2 home win over

Finland in November 1993, and also netted in the following year's World Cup finals third place play-off against Bulgaria in Los Angeles, when the Swedes ran out comfortable 4–0 victors.

When Wim Jansen left for Japan, Henrik failed to get on with the new Feyenoord coach Arie Haan, who would frequently substitute him or leave him on the bench. So when his mentor Jansen arrived in Paradise he instantly sought out his prodigy. Henrik had a clause in his club contract which gave him the right to leave Holland if a foreign outfit were willing to pay a fee of £650,000 (the asking price for any interested Dutch side was £1.8m). Unfortunately, Feyenoord tried to block his move to Celtic and Larsson had to take the Rotterdam giants to court to get his freedom.

After a shaky start to his Celtic career he soon won over the supporters with his skill, strength and goalscoring exploits. On the final day of the 1997/98 campaign, against St Johnstone at a packed Parkhead, Celtic needed to win to

The deadly Henrik Larsson shoots for goal.

claim the League title for the first time in ten years. And it was Henrik Larsson who settled the side after a nervy opening couple of minutes with a quite exquisite curling right foot shot from the far corner of the penalty box beyond the 'keeper.

Brilliant at reading situations, Larsson can close on a defender in a split second, and is unselfish in his raids on goal, always playing for the team rather than himself. Crowned the country's best player in 1999 by the SPFA and Scottish Football Writers, he won both these awards again in 2001.

Disaster struck at 7.42 p.m. on Tuesday 21 October 1999 in a UEFA Cup tie in Lyon against Olympique when he suffered the most horrendous of injuries as his tibia snapped. Thankfully, the man who celebrates scoring a goal by amusingly sticking his tongue out bounced back better than ever. He scored and was named Man of the Match in Sweden's Euro 2000 group game against Italy, but his

country failed to advance to the next stage of the competition.

In 2000/01 he set a Scottish post-war record of 53 goals as Celtic took the treble, and in the process won for himself UEFA's golden boot. He also hit four goals, which included a hat-trick of penalties, in Sweden's 6–0 2002 World Cup qualifier victory over Moldova. Having netted 24 times in 72 appearances for his country, he quit international football in despair after Sweden were sent spinning out of the 2002 World Cup on the Golden Goal by Senegal, but returned to net twice in Euro 2004 against Bulgaria. 'The Magnificent Seven' scored a brace of goals in the UEFA Cup final in 2003 and in the following year's Scottish Cup final triumph over Dunfermline. After a testimonial against Seville he signed for Barcelona in the summer of 2004. In 2005 he was awarded and accepted an honorary degree by the University of Strathclyde in recognition of his contribution to sport and his impact on Glasgow.

# Bobby Lennox
Forward 1961-1980

| | Appearances | Goals |
|---|---|---|
| League | 297 (50) | 168 |
| Scottish Cup | 47 (5) | 31 |
| League Cup | 107 (14) | 63 |
| Europe | 54 (12) | 14 |
| Other Competitions | 25 (3) | 22 |
| TOTAL | 530 (84) | 298 |

Nicknamed 'Buzz Bomb' (speed), 'Chimp'(ears) and 'Lemon'(misprint), Saltcoats lad Bobby Lennox began his long and distinguished playing career with the Ardrossan side Star of the Sea, alongside his brothers Allan and Eric, and Roy Aitken's father.

After a spell with a junior club, Ardeer Recreation, he signed provisional forms for Celtic in September 1961 and in March of the following year he made his debut at inside right against Dundee. Training on the heavy going Saltcoats sands made him light-footed on grass and ultimately a very fast attacker. He would spring forward like a gazelle and his acceleration was such that Jock Stein often complained of linesmen being too slow and wrongly giving 'Lemon' offside when he had in fact sprinted into space.

It was Bobby who scored with the vital second strike for Scotland 12 minutes from time to defeat England at Wembley in 1967, and he collected 10 international caps in total. Arsenal manager Bertie Mee offered a British record fee for his signature in the late 1960s, but Stein did not tell Lennox of the Gunners' interest.

He scored in three consecutive Scottish Cup finals (1969–71), and is in second place to Larsson's postwar goal-scoring record. On New Year's Day 1974 versus Clyde he was booked for the first time in 12 years (his ordering off *v.* Racing Club was a case of mistaken identity).He hit a hat-trick for Bobby Charlton's Select XI in a testimonial match for Liverpool's Tommy Smith at Anfield in May 1977, and in 1978 he starred in the NASL for Houston Hurricanes before returning to help Celtic take the League title in 1979. Lennox retired in 1980 to become Celts reserve team coach.

His teammate Bobby Murdoch described him as 'a happy-go-lucky type who is always laughing and singing the latest hit record', while fellow goalscoring great Jimmy Greaves said of 'Buzz Bomb': 'I liked his direct style of play. He was jet-paced, and could finish electrifying runs with precise centres or fierce shots. Bobby has been a model professional, with a dedication and loyalty that should be an example to all aspiring young footballers. He thoroughly deserved his award of the MBE in 1981 for his unselfish services to the game.'

|  | Appearances | Goals |
|---|---|---|
| **League** | 254 | 26 |
| **Scottish Cup** | 51 | 2 |
| **Glasgow Cup** | 32 | 0 |
| **Charity Cup** | 21 | 5 |
| **Other Competitions** | 34 | 1 |
| **TOTAL** | 392 | 34 |

Strong, reliable central defender Willie Loney was broad shouldered and a granite hard tackler who could use the ball intelligently and occasionally foraged forward to have a pop at goal with his blockbuster shot. Loney began his career with a local junior outfit, Denny Athletic, and signed for Celtic at the turn of the century. Dubbed the 'Obliterator', he was a member of arguably the finest-ever half-back line (Young, Loney and Hay) and partnered club-mate Jimmy Hay in both his internationals for Scotland against Ireland and Wales in 1910.

He made a goal-scoring debut for Celtic in a 2–0 win over Hearts on 17 September 1900, and soon became a sound and consistent pivot who always dominated his area of the pitch. In those days Celtic played all their football on the carpet and when Loney once inadvertently lobbed a high ball to Jimmy McMenemy, repartee ensued. An indignant 'Napoleon' shouted back to him, 'Did you think I brought a ladder?' Willie replied, ' Do you expect me to put it in your pocket?'

In the autumn of 1913 he joined Motherwell and almost immediately got into trouble with the Fir Park board of directors after being absent from training for a week following a 5–0 beating by Clyde. Transferred to Partick Thistle in May 1914 for £40, Loney ended his playing career with Clydebank, whither he had moved after a season at Firhill. Willie Loney gathered a host of honours from the game, including representing the Scottish League and Glasgow. He died on 6 March 1956, aged seventy-six.

# Willie Lyon
Centre half 1935-1940

| | Appearances | Goals |
|---|---|---|
| League | 146 | 16 |
| Scottish Cup | 17 | 1 |
| Glasgow Cup | 10 | 1 |
| Charity Cup | 8 | 1 |
| Other Competitions | 32 | 0 |
| TOTAL | 213 | 19 |

A ferociously effective centre half signed from the senior amateurs Queen's Park in 1935, Willie Lyon was that rare breed: a 'Spider' who made it in Paradise. A stubborn pivot brilliant in heading, positioning and marshalling his defence, Birkenhead-born Lyon was a magnificent captain who brought some much needed stability to the Celtic rearguard, and in his initial season the club registered their first League title success in a decade. This triumph was followed up by the Scottish Cup in 1937 and the League Championship and Empire Exhibition Trophy in 1938 – with Charity Cup wins in 1936, 1937 and 1938 for good measure.

As a centre half, Lyon made for a commanding figure on the football field, who lived up to his name with courage and power to become an inspirational influence capable of exerting authority over many young colleagues like Paterson, MacDonald, Crum, Delaney, Buchan and Divers. Alongside Geatons and Paterson, he formed a fearsome half-back line which revived something of the glory days of Young, Loney and Hay.

Whilst serving in the Royal Artillery during the Second World War, he was awarded the Military Cross for bravery. He entered the war a private and came out a major, having seen action in North Africa, taken part in the landings in Sicily in 1943, and been wounded in Normandy in 1944.

Willie Lyon was assistant-manager of Dundee during the 1947/48 season, and when he died in Salford on 5 December 1962 flags flew at half-mast and players wore black armbands at Paradise to commemorate his early death at the age of fifty. His brother Tom played with Chesterfield and also made a few appearances for Celtic at the beginning of the unofficial wartime campaign.

# Dan McArthur
Goalkeeper 1892-1903

| | Appearances | Shut-outs |
|---|---|---|
| League | 104 | 33 |
| Scottish Cup | 19 | 8 |
| Glasgow Cup | 22 | 4 |
| Charity Cup | 13 | 5 |
| Other Competitions | 35 | 7 |
| TOTAL | 193 | 57 |

Celtic's first great goalkeeper, wee Dan McArthur, stood barely 5ft 6in tall in his stocking soles and weighed only 10st, yet his lack of stature did not prevent him from displaying a marvellous agility and acrobatic nimbleness which gained him international recognition and all the game's honours. Born in Old Monkland in Lanarkshire on 9 August 1867, he made the senior grade from Parkhead Juniors fairly late in life and was already twenty-five years old when he appeared for his Celtic debut in a 3–2 home League win over Abercorn on 10 September 1892. A brave little fellow, McArthur was always in the thick of the action and was often injured as a result. In the Glasgow Cup semi-final against Queen's Park at Hampden in 1896/97, he sustained the first

of several head injuries in his career and ended that match swathed in bandages after a fearless dive at an opponent's feet.

Although regarded by many as the best custodian in Scotland, being both alert and consistently brilliant, he received a meagre three caps for his country. The first of these was at the magnificent new 'Garden of Paradise', Celtic Park, on 30 March 1895, and saw Ireland on the wrong end of a 3–1 scoreline. A week later, the Scots lost 3–0 at Liverpool against England, but Dan had a fine outing and was exempt of any blame. He kept a clean sheet in his last international appearance against Wales at Wrexham four years later as Scotland slew the Dragons 6–0.

Dan's downfall came in the 1901 Scottish Cup final with an awful display in Celts' 4–3 defeat by Hearts, and he conceded a further three goals to Third Lanark the following month in the Charity Cup final. Scotland's smallest 'keeper, McArthur moved to Clyde in 1903. He died on 11 November 1943.

## Andy McAtee
Outside right 1910-1924

| | Appearances | Goals |
|---|---|---|
| League | 406 | 73 |
| Scottish Cup | 32 | 4 |
| Glasgow Cup | 24 | 3 |
| Charity Cup | 22 | 6 |
| Other Competitions | 11 | 7 |
| TOTAL | 495 | 93 |

With legs like a billiard table, right-sided winger Andy McAtee had tremendous speed off the mark and an incredibly powerful shot. Born at Cumbernauld in the summer of 1888, Andy began his career with minor teams Croy Celtic and Mossend Hibs. On entering the gates of Paradise in 1910, he struck up a unique understanding with the great Patsy Gallagher on the right flank, and between them they helped the Hoops overwhelm opponents week after week. This almost telepathic partnership with Patsy saw Celtic collect a large haul of honours before, during and after the First World War.

McAtee won only one full cap for Scotland, against Wales at Wrexham on 3 March 1913, but made a further seven starts for the Scottish League as well as representing Glasgow against Sheffield. He worked in the coalmines for much of the war, before spending the last year of the conflict in uniform as a gunner in the Italian Alps.

When Celtic regained the League Championship in 1918/19, Andy was in fantastic form in the vital run-in. In a 3-2 win at Tynecastle in the penultimate fixture of the campaign – he scored one and created the other two; and before a record crowd at Ayr in the final match he netted a wonderful strike and laid on another for McLean in a 2-0 victory which saw Celts take the title just one point ahead of Rangers. However, perhaps the ultimate moment of joy in Andy McAtee's career came at Cappielow on a spring afternoon in 1922. With Celtic needing a point to be crowned Champions, Morton led 1-0, and as the game entered its dying minutes the goalie Edwards fumbled a high cross ball and handy Andy headed home to secure the League flag. McAtee sailed to the USA in 1925, where he played for Charlie Shaw's New Bedford FC. He died at Condorrot on 15 July 1956. His nephew, Tony McAtee, played for Celtic during the Second World War.

# Frank McAvennie

Striker 1987-1989, 1992-1993

| | Appearances | Goals |
|---|---|---|
| League | 82 (3) | 37 |
| Scottish Cup | 10 | 4 |
| League Cup | 7 | 8 |
| Europe | 4 | 1 |
| Other Competitions | 1 | 0 |
| TOTAL | 104 (3) | 50 |

'Peroxide Playboy' and supersonic striker Frank McAvennie entered the professional game late in life when he signed for St Mirren a fortnight before his twenty-first birthday in November 1980 from Johnstone Burgh. Having previously been a Partick Thistle trialist, Frank had several jobs (including as a road digger with the black stuff) before making the grade at Love Street. With brilliant heading ability and an explosive shot, he was scooped up by West Ham United in the summer of 1985 for £340,000. At Upton Park he proved the perfect foil for Tony Cottee and had a marvellous first season, scoring 26 goals in 41 games, as the Hammers raced to their best-ever position, third in the old First Division. Such remarkable marksmanship earned him an international call-up and a lovely goal against Australia in the World Cup play-off at Hampden.

The bright lights of London certainly appealed to McAvennie, and he regularly attended West End night spots with Page three beauties on his arm. However, the goals dried up in the following 1986/87 campaign, and he registered a mere 7 in 36 League outings.

Transferred to Celtic in October 1987 for £750,000, the move revived McAvennie's goalscoring touch and his partnership with Andy Walker was regarded as the deadliest in Scottish football. 'Macca' netted twice in the 1988 Scottish Cup final as Celtic lifted the double, but he disappointed the faithful support by returning to London in March 1989 for £1.25 million.

His move back to Parkhead in February 1993 showed he had lost none of his poaching instincts, albeit in a poorer team. Subsequent month-long loans and trials with Swindon Town, Airdrie, Falkirk and St Mirren were fruitless and he retired in 1995. Since then his life has spiralled downwards, and he was recently cleared of well-publicised drugs charges. He had a benefit match between St Mirren Legends and Celtic Legends on 13 October 2002 at Love Street, and the following year his autobiography was appropriately entitled *Scoring: An Expert's Guide*.

## Joe McBride
### Striker, 1965-1968

| | Appearances | Goals |
|---|---|---|
| League | 52 (3) | 54 |
| Scottish Cup | 8 | 3 |
| League Cup | 21 | 24 |
| Europe | 10 | 5 |
| Other Competitions | 3 | 2 |
| TOTAL | 94 (3) | 88 |

A typically sharp opportunist who scored with both feet and his head, the 'Govan Goals Machine' and man of many clubs, Joe McBride, was an extrovert character with a cheerful personality who fitted into the Parkhead set-up perfectly when he signed for £22,000 in the summer of 1965. Born in Glasgow on 10 June 1938, Joe had done the rounds playing for Kilmarnock, Wolves, Luton, Partick Thistle and Motherwell before becoming Jock Stein's first signing. He finished his inaugural season with Celtic as top marksman with 31 goals in 30 League games, The following term he had hit an amazing 18 goals from only 14 starts in the League, and an equally astounding 15 goals in 10 League Cup fixtures when his knee gave way on 24 December 1966 against Aberdeen.

Capped twice by Scotland against Wales and Northern Ireland in the autumn of 1966, he netted a hat-trick in the Scottish League's 6–0 victory over the League of Ireland at Celtic Park before injury prematurely ended his international career.

On 5 November 1968, McBride was transferred to Hibernian for £15,000. At Easter Road he continued to show his natural-born prowess as a goalscorer by topping Hibs' charts in both the 1968/69 and 1969/70 campaigns. He cost Dunfermline Athletic a paltry £4,000 in December 1970, and then joined Clyde in October 1971 before retiring the following year. Jimmy McGrory regarded Joe as 'the best Celtic centre forward I've ever seen', while Jock Stein defined him as 'the quintessential striker; the kind of player who, when he didn't know what else to do with the ball, stuck it in the net'.

He ran the Wee Mill Bar next to Shawfield Stadium in Rutherglen on retirement. His son, Joe junior, played for Everton, Rotherham, Oldham, Hibs, Dundee and East Fife, as well as for Scotland at under-21 level.

| | Appearances | Goals |
|---|---|---|
| League | 129 (16) | 99 |
| Scottish Cup | 14 (4) | 11 |
| League Cup | 19 (1) | 9 |
| Europe | 14 (3) | 3 |
| Other Competitions | 4 | 3 |
| TOTAL | 180 (24) | 125 |

University student Brian McClair dropped out of college to concentrate on a full-time football career with Celtic. A prolific marksman and an intelligent linkman, 'Choccy' was Billy McNeill's last signing when he came to Parkhead from Motherwell for £75,000 in June 1983, having previously been on the books of Aston Villa.

It seemed a tall order for him to wear Charlie Nicholas' shooting boots, but McClair fitted into them with commendable comfort. Indeed, he topped Celts' goalscoring charts for four consecutive seasons and gained international caps in the process.

The author and a friend approached Brian at a Pogues pop concert, the evening after Jock Stein's untimely death at Cardiff in 1985, with the demand that he score a goal for the 'Big Man' that coming Saturday against Aberdeen. 'Choccy' replied: 'I'll score two.' He was as good as his word – Celtic won 2–1 and his second

goal duly arrived in 88 minutes when McClair powerfully headed home Provan's corner.

Voted Scotland's Player of the Year in 1987, he moved to Manchester United that summer for an £850,000 fee decided by tribunal, after Celtic had reportedly valued him at £2 million. McClair was an immediate success at Old Trafford, and in his first campaign became the first Man United player since George Best in 1967/68 to reach 20 League goals in a single season. He scored the only goal of the 1992 League Cup final against Nottingham Forest, appropriately his 100th goal for United, and also netted his first goal for Scotland against the CIS in the European Championship in Sweden that same year. When Eric Cantona arrived in November 1992, McClair moved back into a midfield role. Under Fergie he won all the honours the English game had to offer, made over 400 appearances and scored 126 goals.

Capped on 30 occasions, in July 1998 he went back to Motherwell on a free transfer and later that year joined Brian Kidd's coaching staff at Blackburn Rovers.

# Jimmy McColl

Centre forward 1913-1920

| | Appearances | Goals |
|---|---|---|
| League | 165 | 117 |
| Scottish Cup | 4 | 6 |
| Glasgow Cup | 7 | 1 |
| Charity Cup | 7 | 7 |
| Other Competitions | 5 | 2 |
| TOTAL | 188 | 133 |

One of only a dozen or so players to have scored over a century of League goals for Celtic, Jimmy McColl arrived at Parkhead from St Anthony's in 1913. Drafted in at centre forward to replace the disappointing Englishman Ebenezer Owers for the Scottish Cup final replay of 16 April 1914 against Hibernian, McColl netted twice in Celts' convincing 4–1 victory. A tough and sturdy little fellow, Jimmy's tenacity brought dividends and he finished the club's top goalscorer in four of the next five seasons.

The only blight on this remarkable record came when he missed most of the 1917/18 campaign. In November 1917 he had to undergo an operation for appendicitis and took a long time to recover his fitness. He had barely been restored to the side before a twisted knee sustained in a 3–1 defeat at home to Third Lanark on 23 March 1918 put him out of action for the rest of the season. In 1919 there was a new kid on the block, ironically enough also from the 'Ants', named Tommy McInally and 'McColl the Sniper' lost his place in the starting line-up.

He moved to Stoke City in the summer of 1920 for the then astronomical sum of £2,250, but his wife failed to settle in the Potteries and he returned to Scotland the following year to sign for Partick Thistle. Easter Road boss Alec Maley admired McColl, so the 'cash-strapped stony-faced Irish directors of Hibernian made every penny available to get Jimmy' in October 1922. Although he had brief interludes with Leith Athletic and Belfast Celtic in the early 1930s, Hibs presented him with a gold watch to mark fifty years' service to the club as player, trainer and general assistant in a public ceremony at the ground on 2 August 1971. The first man to score 100 League and cup goals for the Edinburgh outfit, he died aged eighty-five in March 1978.

## Utility 1932-1945

|  | Appearances | Goals |
| --- | --- | --- |
| League | 136 | 31 |
| Scottish Cup | 13 | 6 |
| Glasgow Cup | 11 | 1 |
| Charity Cup | 10 | 1 |
| Other Competitions | 220 | 18 |
| TOTAL | 390 | 57 |

Malcolm MacDonald was an extremely gifted footballer of some class and grace, who could play in most positions. Indeed, by the time he left Celtic, Malky had been used in every outfield position, and such was his natural talent that he never looked uncomfortable, no matter where he was asked to perform.

Glasgow-born MacDonald signed for Celtic in 1930 and was farmed out to St Anthony's to gain experience before a sudden change in his fortunes within a week in April 1932 saw him star in a schools match at centre half and then outside left for Celtic in a League game at Firhill. The versatile fellow scored twice on his Hoops debut, despite having never played on the left flank before. The very next week, Celts were back in Maryhill for a Charity Cup tie against

the Jags and again he netted a brace. Malky, or Calum as team-mates and fans liked to call him, had two terms at centre half but moved to inside forward when Willie Lyon arrived from Queen's Park in 1935. A member of the Glory team of 1938, MacDonald represented Scotland at both school and junior level, and also appeared in three wartime internationals with one outing for the Scottish League. He subsequently played for and managed both Kilmarnock and Brentford, and even had a brief spell as caretaker manager of Scotland in the mid-1960s.

Calum's reflections on his days with Celtic indicated just how much wearing the Hooped jersey had meant to him: 'I look back with great affection on the fourteen years I spent with the club and the wonderful colleagues I had there. We were only temporary custodians of Celtic's greatness and they were happy days. I wouldn't change them for anything.' Malcolm MacDonald, a hero to a generation of Celtic supporters, died on 26 September 1999, aged eighty-five.

# Jean McFarlane
Left-half 1919-1929

| | Appearances | Goals |
|---|---|---|
| League | 268 | 12 |
| Scottish Cup | 36 | 2 |
| Glasgow Cup | 20 | 2 |
| Charity Cup | 14 | 0 |
| Other Competitions | 2 | 0 |
| TOTAL | 340 | 16 |

A polished performer at left-half, John 'Jean' McFarlane had tremendous sprinting powers and could kill a descending ball before sweeping past an opponent. His long, raking stride, excellent positional sense and superb control under pressure were all allied to the ability to use the ball effectively (his only weakness, apparently, was 'a touch of apathy on occasion').

Born at Bathgate on 21 November 1899, he joined Celtic from Fife junior side Wellesley and made his debut at outside right in a goalless encounter at Motherwell in April 1920. Initially fielded at inside left – he played in that position when Celtic won the League in 1922 and Scottish Cup in 1923 – he moved back to left-half for the beginning of the 1923/24 campaign. Selected for Bob Kelly's 'best-ever Celtic team', yet incredibly Jean never received a full international cap for Scotland, although he did represent the Scottish League *v.* the Football League in 1925 and 1928, and made a further

two appearances against the Irish League. He transferred to Middlesbrough in the summer of 1929 in a closed season clearance sale at Celtic Park that also saw Willie McStay, the captain and veteran defender, move to Hearts.

Jean made 101 League and cup appearances for the Cleveland club, and signed for the recently promoted Dunfermline Athletic in June 1934, where he teamed up once again with ex-Celt Alec Thomson. McFarlane was known as 'Jean' not because that is the French equivalent of John, but because a female character named Jean McFarlane featured in a popular newspaper serial of the time. He apparently got the nickname from a groundsman at Celtic Park. This exquisite passer of the ball died in February 1956. His younger brother Hugh starred for Hibernian and attended St Andrew's University where he won an MA degree.

# Frank McGarvey

Centre forward 1980-1985

|  | Appearances | Goals |
|---|---|---|
| League | 159 (9) | 77 |
| Scottish Cup | 20 (4) | 13 |
| League Cup | 29 (6) | 11 |
| Europe | 19 | 8 |
| Other Competitions | 2 | 0 |
| TOTAL | 229 (19) | 109 |

A terrace wag once summed up Frank McGarvey's style perfectly: 'Frank disnae know wit he's daen wae the ba', so wit chance has the opposition?' It is true that, at times during a game, McGarvey's legs seemed to be made of rubber as he bent one way and twisted the other, totally deceiving defenders before laying the ball off for a team-mate, or alternatively straightening himself for a blistering shot at goal. 'Squiggles' began his playing career with Coltness YC and starred for Kilsyth Rangers in the 1974/75 season (scoring 15 goals) before signing for St Mirren in the summer of 1975.

As an unorthodox striker, he helped the Paisley outfit take the Scottish First Division title in 1976/77. When he paraded his goalscoring talents on the bigger stage of the Premier League, he inevitably caught the eye of the game's giants and in May 1979 cost Liverpool a reputed £300,000. At Anfield McGarvey never made a single first-team appearance, yet was selected twice by Scotland during this period on Merseyside.

After that wasted year in England, he returned to Scotland and signed for Celtic in March 1980, for a club record fee of £250,000. Always a dangerous raider, McGarvey became the first player to score a century of Premier League goals when he converted a hat-trick for Celts against St Mirren on 24 November 1984. However, amazingly only days after scoring the winner in the 1985 Scottish Cup final against Dundee United, he went to the Buddies for the relatively meagre sum of £75,000.

Frank won a Scottish Cup winner's medal with St Mirren in 1987, was appointed player-manager of Queen of the South in 1990, and in 1992/93 finished top scorer for Clyde with 16 goals, as they captured the Second Division Championship. More recently he had a spell with Shotts Bon Accord, before retiring.

# Peter McGonagle
Left-back 1926-1936

| | Appearances | Goals |
|---|---|---|
| League | 286 | 7 |
| Scottish Cup | 37 | 1 |
| Glasgow Cup | 25 | 1 |
| Charity Cup | 14 | 0 |
| Other Competitions | 3 | 1 |
| TOTAL | 365 | 10 |

The 'Hooded Menace', William McGonagle (called Peter in honour of his father, who played for Hamilton Accies), was an intimidating competitor and formidable full-back who joined Celtic from Duntocher Hibs in 1926. A contemporary appraisal said: 'McGonagle shirks nothing and kicks a thundering ball with either foot. He has highly developed the art of anticipation and can be depended upon never to let his team down.' Peter's tough tackling and committed performances underlined his ability as one of the most sound and consistent players of that period. He sustained a knee injury on 7 April 1928 and, due mainly to his absence, Celtic lost four of their last six fixtures of the 1927/28 campaign – including the 0–4 reverse against Rangers the following week in the Scottish Cup final. His injury later required a cartilage operation.

On his international debut in 1933, Scotland beat England 2–1 at Hampden; he received six caps altogether and also represented the Scottish League five times.

Ordered off against Rangers at Ibrox on New Year's Day 1935, when he foolishly threw the ball at Bob McPhail (having previously been cautioned for a foul on Jimmy Smith), he was so incensed and distraught that referee Mr Craigmyle (Aberdeen) had to 'take him by the arm' off the field. Ten days later a crowd assembled at the SFA offices in Carlton Place waiting to hear the verdict of the Referee Committee. When it was announced that Peter had been fined £20 and suspended for twenty days, there was a moment's silence – and then a hullabaloo! Manager Maley and McGonagle slipped out a back entrance, while the referee Craigmyle got a torrent of abuse from the supporters as he left by the front door. Ironically, Peter's last appearance in the hoops came a full year later in the Ne'erday Old Firm clash at Parkhead. After brief spells with Dunfermline Athletic, Hamilton Accies and Cheltenham, he resumed his trade as a motor mechanic.

# Danny McGrain
Right-back 1967-1987

|  | Appearances | Goals |
| --- | --- | --- |
| League | 433 (8) | 4 |
| Scottish Cup | 60 | 1 |
| League Cup | 105 (1) | 3 |
| Europe | 53 (1) | 0 |
| Other Competitions | 24 (2) | 1 |
| TOTAL | 675 (12) | 9 |

World-class full-back Danny McGrain had an attractive overlapping style which endeared him to the Parkhead faithful. He starred for Glasgow Schools and Scotland Schoolboys and had spells with Drumchapel Amateurs and Queen's Park Victoria XI before Celtic signed Danny in 1967 and farmed him out to Maryhill FC for six months. McGrain bided his time with Celts' successful second string, and after a brief debut as a substitute at Tannadice in a midweek League Cup tie, he made his full first-team start in a 2–0 home win over Morton on 29 August 1970.

Seen as 'Mr Indestructible', throughout his career, Danny triumphantly overcame major setbacks: a fractured skull in March 1972 at Brockville; the discovery that he was a diabetic in the World Cup summer of 1974; and a severe ankle injury in October 1977, which kept him out of the game for eighteen months. Through all this McGrain battled on, and such determination and dedication brought Jock Stein to comment: 'He has been a model professional footballer since the first day he arrived at Celtic Park.' Nobody disagreed with the 'Big Man's' sentiment. The key figure of Celts' double-winning side of 1976/77, he capped a wonderful season by being nominated Writers' Player of the Year and helping Scotland defeat England at Wembley. On the international front, he made his debut in a 2–0 win over Wales at Wrexham in 1973 and always seemed to give wing wizard Leighton James a torrid time; after one game, the contact lens-wearing Welshman accidentally bumped into Danny in the poorly lit tunnel. McGrain turned quickly and jokingly commented to a Scottish journalist: 'See that? He still can't get round me!' Scotland badly missed his qualities in defence in Argentina in 1978, and many, including Sir Alf Ramsey, were of the opinion that Danny McGrain could have made it really big in South America and become a household name throughout the football world. He subsequently captained his country against England in 1981 and 1982, and accumulated a total of 62 caps.

Within months of his return from injury, Celtic clinched the 1978/79 Championship by beating Rangers 4–2 on an unforgettable night in Paradise. He was awarded an MBE in 1983 and Glasgow also honoured him with a civic medal for services to sport on 14 September 1987. That same year he joined Hamilton Accies and won a First Division Championship medal, before becoming a coach at Clydebank. Appointed manager of Arbroath in 1992/93, he became something of a cult figure with the 'Red Lichties' fans, many of whom sported a false moustache and beard at games in his honour.

Until recently he worked in corporate entertainment at the Gleneagles golf course. Danny McGrain's portrait hangs in the National Gallery of Scotland. His father, Robert, played for Hearts around 1945.

# Jimmy McGrory
Centre forward 1922-1937

| | Appearances | Goals |
|---|---|---|
| League | 378 | 397 |
| Scottish Cup | 67 | 75 |
| Glasgow Cup | 35 | 34 |
| Charity Cup | 21 | 21 |
| Other Competitions | I | 0 |
| TOTAL | 502 | 527 |

Jimmy McGrory is the greatest scorer in the history of British football. He netted Celts' winner in the 1925 and 1933 Scottish Cup finals, and also found the target in the 1931 final and replay. His 550 goals are the record aggregate figure for the British game; he scored an astonishing 410 goals in only 408 League matches, another record; his 8 goals against Dunfermline Athletic in January 1928 is a feat that has never been equalled in Scottish League football; and his three-minute hat-trick against Motherwell on 14 March 1936 is still the quickest in the League.

Born and raised in the tough Garngad area of Glasgow, McGrory had none of the coarseness so often assumed in such an environment. He initially starred with local team St Roch's and scored in the 1922 Scottish Junior Cup final success over Kilwinning Rangers. After signing for Celtic, he was loaned to Clydebank and finished the 1923/24 season as their top marksman with 13 goals, before returning to help Celtic win the Charity Cup in May 1924. Broad-shouldered and deep chested, McGrory developed an almost telepathic understanding with team-mates through the 1920s and 1930s. In 1933 Jimmy started the famous 'Hampden Roar' from a Bob McPhail pass as Scotland defeated England, having already scored against the 'Auld Enemy' two years previously. Capped

on a mere seven occasions, he also represented the Scottish League six times.

He converted chances with either foot, but his outstanding feature was the incredible power and accuracy of his heading. On one notable occasion the Queen's Park 'keeper Jack Harkness broke three fingers trying to stop a McGrory header. Although nobody bothered to keep a tally in those days, it is generally believed that almost half of his 500-plus competitive goals were scored with the head, although none of McGrory's record 8 against Dunfermline came via that 'Golden Crust'. Not surprisingly, such domination in the air meant that his skills on the ground were often overlooked, and in his early days at Parkhead this led to him being nicknamed the 'Mermaid'. Indeed, speaking of such awesome heading ability, that great wit and

Celtic legend Jimmy McGrory commiserates with Aberdeen skipper Eddie Falloon at the end of the 1937 Scottish Cup final. Hampden Park was crammed with 146,433 spectators, still a record for a club match in Europe.

ex-Celt Tommy McInally once said: 'They didnae lace up Jimmy's boots before a game, they laced up his heid and threw him on to the park.'

In the 1935/36 campaign, McGrory topped the League's goalscoring charts with 50 conversions, and shortly after Celtic captured the Scottish Cup in 1937 this all-time great retired. Jimmy McGrory would have regarded the thought of leaving Celtic as sacrilege and when his boss Willie Maley tried to sell him to Herbert Chapman's Arsenal for a record fee in 1928, the player fought hard in a bid to remain at Parkhead. He was appointed manager of Kilmarnock in December 1937, a post he held until he took over as Celtic boss in July 1945. This legendary figure in the annals of the club died in Glasgow on 20 October 1982, aged seventy-eight.

# Tommy McInally
Centre forward 1919-1922, Inside left 1925-1928

| | Appearances | Goals |
|---|---|---|
| League | 188 | 112 |
| Scottish Cup | 25 | 16 |
| Glasgow Cup | 16 | 8 |
| Charity Cup | 9 | 6 |
| Other Competitions | 2 | 2 |
| TOTAL | 240 | 144 |

A jovial jester and fabulous footballer, Tommy McInally signed for Celtic from St Anthony's in 1919. A slim Barrhead boy with lightning fast speed ( a fact demonstrated by his beating of the famous W.B. Applegarth in a sprint in October 1920), Tommy scored a hat-trick on his debut against Clydebank on 16 August 1919 and topped the goalscoring charts in his first season at Parkhead with over 30 goals in all competitions. Neighbour and idol of future Rangers legend Bob McPhail ('When I saw him in the street or travelled on the same tramcar I would look at him in awe'), McInally continued to find the net on a regular basis for another two terms before being sold to Third Lanark in September 1922 for a substantial fee.

Having toured Argentina in the summer of 1923 with the 'Warriors', he returned to Paradise in 1925, not as the quicksilver striker of yesteryear, but as an influential inside forward, and with a stable side Celts raced to the League title in 1926. However, his aversion to training, along with weight and discipline problems, took its toll on the club, who offloaded him in the closed season of 1928 to Sunderland for £2,500.

Two episodes during his last year with Celtic are worth recalling, as they ultimately led to his departure south of the border. Celtic were drawn away to Keith in the second round of the Scottish Cup and the players had heard that a tailor in the town had promised a new suit to any member of the Keith side who scored a goal against the mighty Celtic. So, with the Bhoys winning convincingly, McInally got possession of the ball, duly dribbled back through his own team-mates and laid a lovely pass to the Keith striker's feet, who wasted no time dispatching the ball past Celts' 'keeper and won himself a brand-new made-to-measure suit. Tommy also failed to return home with the official party and instead stayed behind to sample the Highland hospitality – an indulgence which lasted some three days! Prior to the quarter-final of the same competition at Motherwell, he walked out of training at Seamill, after his colleagues had played the old newspaper-reporter-on-the-phone trick against him, and didn't return that week. The board suspended him 'for breach of training rules and disobedience'- his days in Glasgow's East End were numbered.

Capped twice by Scotland, he won League Championship badges in 1922 and 1926 and a Scottish Cup winner's medal in 1927. His popularity with the Parkhead faithful was immeasurable. A fireman told of the time he was called to deal with a flood in a Glasgow tenement. He pulled out an old Irishman but

Prankster Tommy McInally (far right) looks on as John Thomson makes a save during the 1928 Scottish Cup final against Rangers.

was shocked to hear him moan, 'Oh, dear, poor Tommy McInally's getting all wet. Save Tommy. Don't let Tommy get wet.' The fireman darted back inside the room and was confronted by a huge picture of Tommy McInally above the old man's bed. Jimmy McGrory recalled: 'Tommy was fond of a wee drink and this is what led to an incident at the seamill Hydrom which was a temperance hotel, where we were again on special training. The Hydro was a very quiet place and most of the guests were elderly people. One night around 10 p.m. Tommy was at a loose end as we sar beside the bottom of the main stairway chatting. Suddenly he produced a half-bottle of whisky and I just about dropped dead with fright in case Mr Maley was around. I think Tommy must have already had a gulp or two because he was in one of his practical jokes mood. He noticed some of the old people filling cups from a hot water container to take with them to their rooms. Suddenly he told me: "I think I'll liven up that water a bit and give the old folks a treat." For God's sake Tommy, don't do that. It'll cause a riot." But he was determined to go ahead. More old people came along to fill their cups and we sat there to watch the outcome. Within minutes we were roaring with laughter in a corner as most of the bedroom doors began to open and most of the folk came back down for a second helping of what must have been the drink of water they had ever had!' Stories about McInally are endless. Apparently once he asked the referee for his whistle and blew for a foul against himself. His subsequent sojourns took him to Bournemouth (November 1929), Morton (1930) and Derry City (January 1931).

# Duncan MacKay
Right-back, 1955-1964

| | Appearances | Goals |
|---|---|---|
| League | 162 | 5 |
| Scottish Cup | 33 | 2 |
| League Cup | 37 | 0 |
| Europe | 4 | 0 |
| Other Competitions | 18 | 0 |
| TOTAL | 254 | 7 |

Classy right-back Duncan MacKay attended St Columba of Iona secondary school and starred for local sides St Mary's Boys' Guild and Maryhill Harp before entering Paradise with his team-mate Bertie Auld in April 1955. MacKay spent his first few seasons at Parkhead as a wing-half in reserve-team football, but after moving to full-back his career reached new heights. He made his debut in a League Cup tie against Clyde at Shawfield on 9 August 1958 and so rapid was his progress that towards the end of his first season he played for Scotland against England at Wembley.

A swift sweeping defender with good positional sense, Dunky excelled as an overlapping full-back before that style of play became fashionable, and made the right-back berth, for club and country, his own for the next few seasons. Appointed Celts' skipper after Bertie Peacock departed in 1961, MacKay's Parkhead career was surprisingly cut short when he moved to Third Lanark on 6 November 1964 after losing his place in the team to Ian Young. Capped fourteen times for Scotland with a further four appearances at under-23 level, Dunky was unfortunate to be at Celtic Park during a lean period in the club's history, and won little in the way of domestic honours with just two appearances in losing Scottish Cup final sides, in 1961 and 1963, to show for his efforts.

Duncan MacKay emigrated to Australia in the summer of 1965, when he was appointed player-coach of the Melbourne team, Croatia. He returned to Scotland in 1972, coaching the junior outfit St Anthony's while working as manager of a Glasgow manufacturing firm. Subsequently he moved back Down Under to coach South Melbourne.

# Adam McLean
Outside left 1917-1928

|  | Appearances | Goals |
|---|---|---|
| League | 367 | 128 |
| Scottish Cup | 41 | 19 |
| Glasgow Cup | 26 | 9 |
| Charity Cup | 18 | 4 |
| Other Competitions | 6 | 1 |
| TOTAL | 458 | 161 |

Small, light and dainty, Adam McLean was a tantalising left-winger who developed the happy knack of scoring important goals for Celtic: perhaps slight in physique he was a clever and assertive performer nonetheless. Brought up in Greenock, he supported Morton before moving to Belfast when still a boy. He returned to Clydeside and began his playing career with the juvenile side Anderston Thornbank, before joining Celtic in 1917. McLean later recalled the welcome he received: 'I'll never forget the greeting I got when I arrived at Celtic Park for the first time. I didn't even know where the players entered the ground. I had been told to report for my first game (against Dumbarton) and I was wandering about like a lost boy. Suddenly, from near what I learned was the old pavilion, there was a terrible shout. "What's your name?", said the voice, and when I answered, he roared over to another big broad man – "Here's the so and so!" Afterwards I discovered that the questioner was former Celtic full-back Jerry Reynolds, who had been told to watch out for the new player by the man who was to be my boss for twelve years. Willie Maley was the other big man.'

Wee Adam became an integral part of the fine Celtic team of the 1920s and was good enough to force the 'Wee Blue Devil' Alan Morton out of the Scotland side on occasions. As a polished performer down the flank, fed by McInally and McFarlane, he provided a plentiful supply of accurate crosses to boost McGrory's goals tally.

In August 1928, after a dispute over terms, McLean left Parkhead reluctantly, to join up with Tommy McInally at Sunderland. He returned north to sign for Aberdeen in late 1930 before being transferred to Partick Thistle during the 1933 close season.

Appointed the Jags' assistant-trainer in November 1938, he was on their staff for many years, eventually becoming head trainer and then assistant manager for a time from the summer of 1962. Adam McLean received four full Scotland caps and represented the Scottish League on three occasions; he also won three Championship and Scottish Cup medals apiece. He died on 29 June 1973, aged seventy-four.

# Murdo MacLeod
Midfielder 1978-1987

| | Appearances | Goals |
|---|---|---|
| League | 274 (7) | 55 |
| Scottish Cup | 36 (2) | 7 |
| League Cup | 44 | 13 |
| Europe | 33 | 8 |
| Other Competitions | 11 | 0 |
| TOTAL | 398 (9) | 83 |

A launcher of fierce shots and described neatly as 'a mix of non-stop running and bustling aggression', the powerhouse left-sided midfielder Murdo MacLeod received the appropriate nickname of 'Rhino' by the supporters. A product of Glasgow Amateurs, he started his professional career with Dumbarton in 1974 and made his League debut against Queen of the South in October 1975. While with the 'Sons of the Rock', Murdo made 78 League outings and netted twice.

MacLeod's goals tally changed for the better when he was transferred to Celtic in November 1978 for a fee of £100,000, and in his first season – along with another new signing in Kilmarnock's Davie Provan – he played a major role in Celtic's winning the 1978/79 Premier Championship. In the last game of that campaign against Rangers at Parkhead, MacLeod brilliantly hammered home Celts' fourth and final goal to take the title. It was just one of a number of long-range spectacular and vital efforts he would score for the club in the coming years.

The year 1983 saw his name linked with a possible move to Rangers, but he re-signed just as manager Billy McNeill was on the brink of leaving Celtic Park. Murdo eventually moved in the summer of 1987 to the Bundesliga with Borussia Dortmund, and did his bit from time to time as a football pundit for German television.

He starred for Scotland in the World Cup finals of Italia '90, and was temporarily knocked out when a Branco free-kick for Brazil crashed into the Scots' defensive wall. MacLeod gathered 20 full caps in total. In October 1990 he returned home to join Hibernian as player-coach, and won a Skol League Cup winner's medal with the Edinburgh club before going to Dumbarton in 1993. He subsequently became manager at Dumbarton and Partick Thistle, and was assistant to Wim Jansen for Celts' successful 1997/98 campaign. He now runs a restaurant and is a football pundit for BBC Scotland.

# Sandy McMahon
Forward 1890-1903

|  | Appearances | Goals |
|---|---|---|
| League | 176 | 126 |
| Scottish Cup | 43 | 41 |
| Glasgow Cup | 39 | 25 |
| Charity Cup | 17 | 15 |
| Other Competitions | 36 | 10 |
| TOTAL | 311 | 217 |

The first man to score 100 League goals for Celtic, Selkirk-born inside left Sandy McMahon gave long and splendid service to the club after arriving at Parkhead from Hibernian in December 1890. A former painter and plasterer, Sandy broke his time to take up a career in football. Previously with Darlington St Augustines and Burnley, McMahon was a tall, ungainly-looking individual, whose build belied his ability to glide and weave his way through defences.

He had a perfect understanding with Johnny Campbell and between them they bewildered defenders with accurate inter-passing and thunderous shooting. Known as the 'Prince of Dribblers' and the 'Duke', he was also the greatest header of a ball that the Celtic team had seen until the arrival of the equally legendary Jimmy McGrory in the 1920s.

At the height of his powers, a letter arrived informing the club that McMahon and Neilly McCallum had been lured to Nottingham Forest. Celtic representatives were hastily despatched with orders to bring back the 'Duke' at all costs. Forest decided to hide McMahon until the agents got tired of trying to locate him and he could turn out for the English club, thus committing himself to them. However, Sandy was traced and, now apparently delighted to return home, eluded his escort and made a cab and train dash back to Glasgow, where Willie Maley, Celts' match secretary, had alerted the press of the news of the mission's success, thus ensuring a big crowd at the station to welcome the wanderer home.

An intelligent and literate man, McMahon joined Partick Thistle on leaving Celtic in 1903. He had gained four League Championship badges and three Scottish Cup winner's medals, as well as playing six times for Scotland, eight times for the Scottish League and twice for Glasgow against Sheffield. The *Scottish Sport* claimed: 'He was the finest inside left in Britain, and the mainspring of both Campbell and Madden's effectiveness.'

Messrs Tom Campbell and Pat Woods' excellent *The Glory and The Dream* said of Sandy: 'He did have a natural dignity, and, although a most modest and retiring personality, he could be persuaded at club concerts and sing-songs to entertain. Surprisingly his party-piece consisted

'Duke' McMahon, standing back row, centre, in this photo of Celtic's Scottish Cup-winning team of 1899.

of lengthy excerpts from Shakespeare's plays recited with gusto in the approved manner of the famous actor-managers and to an appreciative audience of fellow players and club officials.' Sandy McMahon, hero to the first generation of Celtic supporters, died in Glasgow on 25 January 1916 while still in his mid-forties. "Man In The Know" wrote an obituary tribute in the *Glasgow Observer* from which the following snippet comes: 'It is beyond me to put on record his mystifying gift that amounted to genius. I can only repeat there never was such a wonderful player in all the history of the game,

nor are we ever likely to see his equal. He was unique, unapproachable, literally and figuratively, the last word in scientific football, the delight of spectators, the despair of opponents. To analyse his play, to describe his subtle methods, would take up a good deal of space, even if one were able to explain the incomprehensible. 'Unfortunately he had first one knee then the other put out, to say nothing of an ankle, so that long before his time he had to drop out of the game, leaving behind him a reputation such as no other player is ever likely to gain.

|  | Appearances | Goals |
|---|---|---|
| League | 456 | 144 |
| Scottish Cup | 59 | 24 |
| Glasgow Cup | 43 | 10 |
| Charity Cup | 28 | 11 |
| Other Competitions | 27 | 3 |
| TOTAL | 613 | 192 |

A master strategist who could, and often did, dictate the course of a game with his accurate and telling passes, Jimmy McMenemy is one of the greatest names in the annals of Celtic Football Club. McMenemy orchestrated each Celtic campaign so effectively that he earned himself the appropriate nickname of 'Napoleon'. He possessed a marvellous footballing brain and the football field was his chessboard where his philosophy of 'making the ball do the work' came into force.

Born at Rutherglen, on the outskirts of Glasgow, he starred with his local side Glencairn and worked in a glass factory, and then made chairs, before signing for Celtic in 1902. Almost immediately his generalship qualities came into focus as Celtic entered the finest and most successful period in the club's history. He won a staggering eleven League Championship badges and six Scottish Cup medals – a total that would have surely been more had the Cup competition not been suspended during the First World War.

Capped 12 times by Scotland, at a time when only three international matches were played each season, McMenemy made a further two appearances in the 1919 unofficial victory internationals, as well as representing the Scottish League on fourteen occasions and twice for Glasgow against Sheffield.

In 1920 Celtic stupidly gave him a free transfer to Partick Thistle, and within a season he took the Firhill Jags to the Scottish Cup final, which was ironically staged at Parkhead that year. Their opponents were Rangers and bookmakers gave Thistle no chance. Indeed, some were said to be offering odds of up to 100/1 against them taking the throphy, but with 'Nap' pushed into the side as a late replacement, there was always the prospect of an upset. And it was Jimmy who made the biggest contribution, holding on to the ball, jockeying his fellow attackers into good positions and generally taking the weight off a defence which gave signs that it might collapse. Partick Thistle won 1–0 from a goal by Blair, and McMenemy collected another winner's medal and a considerable sum of money after placing a bet on his side.

He subsequently had a brief spell with Stenhousemuir and was later coach at Partick Thistle and then Celtic. He was the father of several footballing sons: Harry (Newcastle United), John (Celtic, Motherwell and Scotland) and Frank (Hamilton Academical and Northampton Town), while Lawrie McMenemy – a top manager of recent times – is also a distant relative. A truly legendary figure, Jimmy McMenemy died at Robroyston on 23 June 1965.

| | Appearances | Goals |
|---|---|---|
| League | 584 | 8 |
| Scottish Cup | 57 | 0 |
| Glasgow Cup | 45 | 0 |
| Charity Cup | 30 | 0 |
| Other Competitions | 24 | 1 |
| TOTAL | 740 | 9 |

An intelligent, unruffled and extremely well-respected footballer, Alec McNair gave Celtic twenty-one years of sterling service. Born at Bo'ness on Boxing Day 1883, McNair's career began with Stenhousemuir before he arrived at Parkhead in May 1904 on the recommendation of Donny McLeod. After showing his versatility by performing efficiently in a number of positions, he settled in at right-back and remained there with a high degree of success for the rest of his illustrious career. 'Judicious', 'imperturbable', 'shrewd', 'calculating' – these were all adjectives used to describe McNair's thoughtful play and constructive distribution. He was an inspirational figure and his back-passes to goalkeeper Charlie Shaw gave no room for mistakes and ultimately went into the folklore of the game. His coolness under pressure gained him the lasting nickname of the 'Icicle'.

Once, when playing golf, Alec found his ball in a bunker and had difficulty getting it out. Seeing this, a wit from the gallery shouted: 'Pass it back to Charlie, Alec.' For perhaps the only time McNair lost his cool and burst out laughing. On another occasion, Celtic were playing in Dublin and coasting when the opposing centre forward asked McNair to let him score. The veteran defender told the youngster to play up close and that he would give Shaw a short pass back, thus allowing the Irish lad a scoring opportunity. But Charlie Shaw was exceptionally athletic and scooped up the ball, evaded the boy's charge and cleared the danger, leaving McNair to apologise for the brilliance of his 'keeper.

After he retired in 1925, he held the post of secretary-manager with Dundee for two years before becoming a stockbroker in Falkirk.

In his reminiscences of Celtic, manager Willie Maley recorded that McNair was 'a gentleman and a treasure to the club in every way'. He won an incredible eleven League Championship badges (a record), six Scottish Cup winner's medals and fifteen caps for Scotland. Alec also appeared fifteen times for the Scottish League and starred in three victory internationals, as well as once for Glasgow v. Sheffield. He briefly served as an SFA referee inspector before his death at Larbert in November 1951, aged sixty-seven. His son, James, played inside left for Falkirk and Stenhousemuir in the 1930s.

# Jackie McNamara

Defender, Midfielder 1995-2005

|  | Appearances | Goals |
|---|---|---|
| League | 221 (16) | 10 |
| Scottish Cup | 26 (5) | 3 |
| League Cup | 17 (2) | 1 |
| Europe | 43 (9) | 1 |
| Other Competitions | 0 | 0 |
| TOTAL | 307 (32) | 15 |

An excellent acquisition by manager Tommy Burns, Jackie McNamara junior joined Celtic from Dunfermline Athletic on 4 October 1995 at a cost of £600,000, and immediately settled to strike up a telepathic understanding down the right wing with fellow under-21 internationalist Simon Donnelly. Indeed, such a perfect partnership drove Celtic to within touching distance of the League title and won for McNamara the Young Player of the Year award in 1996.

Born in Glasgow on 24 October 1973, Jackie suffered a horrendous career-threatening injury in March 1989 when, during a training session with juvenile side Edina Hibs, his right leg was shattered in two places. Although out of action for seven months, he fought hard to regain his fitness and signed for the Pars on 17 September 1991 from Gairdoch United. Slim, quick and stylish McNamara was moved more into midfield by the astute Wim Jansen, where his accurate passing and skilful, thoughtful play earned him the SPFA Player of the Year accolade in 1997/98, and a spot in Scotland's World Cup squad in France. He replaced the injured Lubo Moravcik during the first half of the 2001 Scottish Cup final at Hampden, and scored the all-important opener to give Celtic the platform from which a 3–0 victory was secured. The longest serving member of the current Celtic team, Jackie took over the club's captaincy from Paul Lambert in 2003/04, and ended the double-winning campaign by being voted the Scottish Football Writers' Association's Player of the Year. Capped 29 times for Scotland, his father, Jackie senior, played for Celtic, Hibernian and Morton. Surprisingly Joined Hoddle's Wolverhampton Wanderers in June 2005 on the Bosman freedom of contract ruling.

# Billy McNeill
Centre half 1957-1975

| | Appearances | Goals |
|---|---|---|
| League | 486 | 22 |
| Scottish Cup | 94 | 7 |
| League Cup | 138 | 4 |
| Europe | 69 | 3 |
| Other Competitions | 40 | 4 |
| TOTAL | 827 | 40 |

One of the most 'decorated' player in British football history, Billy McNeill made the transformation from a crew-cut kid in a struggling Celtic side to the first footballer from these islands to lift the European Cup in 1967. Yet it could all have been so different, for after several seasons of mediocrity at Celtic Park, he was on the verge of leaving the club he loved when Jock Stein arrived as manager in 1965 and changed everything. It was a sight for sore eyes throughout the 1960s and early 1970s, when captain McNeill appeared from the tunnel with an air of invincibility, as he stood tall and thrust out his deep chest, he quite simply oozed confidence and authority.

Born in Bellshill on 2 March 1940, Billy emerged as a strong defender with Our Lady's High School in Motherwell. The son of a soldier, he had previously attended a rugby-playing school in Hereford and was making the grade as a hooker when his father returned to Scotland, where young Billy rediscovered a preference for soccer.

An office junior at an insurance broker's, McNeill was always going to be an outstanding centre half and after only one season with the local side Blantyre Victoria, he arrived at Parkhead in August 1957 for £250. McNeill made his League debut in the second match of the following season, an Old Firm game which ended in a 2–2 draw, and eventually took over

from the legendary Bobby Evans. He was to match his predecessor in both commitment to the club and in durability.

His early days at Parkhead coincided with some gloomy times for Celtic, but after Stein's arrival the club embarked upon an unprecedented run of success and McNeill, a fair-haired, tall, commanding figure in the centre of defence, proved the ideal leader to put Stein's philosophies into practice on the pitch. Superb in the air, he scored some vital goals as Celtic's skipper and won the sports writers' Scottish Player of the Year award in 1965, the year he scored the winning goal in the Scottish Cup final, an event considered by many to be the turning point in the club's history.

'Caesar' passes the Scottish Cup to goalkeeper Denis Connaghan after the 1974 win over Dundee United.

He vied with Rangers' Ronnie McKinnon for the Scotland place and won 29 full caps, which included victories over England at Hampden in 1962 and 1964. He also represented the Scots at under-23 level 5 times and made a further nine appearances for the Scottish League. It was a tribute to his dedication and ability that Tommy Docherty recalled him to strengthen Scotland's defence for the 1972 British Championship.

Nicknamed 'Caesar' (after the actor Cesar Romero rather than the Roman emperor), Billy McNeill played in twenty-four major cup finals and, indeed, his last game for Celtic was the 1975 Scottish Cup final win over Airdrieonians. Awarded the MBE in the Queen's Birthday Honours list of 1974, he subsequently managed Clyde, Aberdeen, Celtic (twice), Manchester City and Aston Villa. However, it is as Celts' captain that the faithful will remember him most of all and the chant from the terraces of 'Oh! There's Only One King Billy, That's McNeill' underlined the affection the supporters had for their 'Caesar'.

| | Appearances | Goals |
|---|---|---|
| League | 141 | 55 |
| Scottish Cup | 23 | 17 |
| League Cup | 37 | 17 |
| Glasgow Cup | 14 | 4 |
| Charity Cup | 12 | 3 |
| Other Competitions | 164 | 15 |
| TOTAL | 391 | 111 |

John McPhail was nicknamed 'Hooky' due to the extraordinary way he used to control and cross the ball with his right foot. A product of St Mungo's Academy, big John played one or two games in Junior football with Ashfield and Blantyre Celtic before entering Paradise in August 1941 from the now defunct Strathclyde club. Born in Lambhill, Glasgow, on 27 December 1923, John McPhail was a lively, courageous bustler with brilliant touches, and was a mainstay of the team for over a decade – with the 1950/51 season perhaps his finest in the green and white hoops.

He scored on his international debut in a 2–0 win over Wales at Hampden in 1949; netted twice in the opening minutes of his third game for Scotland on 1 November 1950 as they thrashed Ireland 6–1; and, within the month, produced the only goal of the game that saw the Scottish League defeat the Football League 1–0 at Ibrox.

However, even though he carried a groin strain for months, he shone the brightest in the Scottish Cup competition that term. After bagging a brace to beat East Fife 4–2 in a first-round replay, he showed his worth again in the third-round tie at Tynecastle when he scored Celts' winner: 'From deep in their own half Tully and McPhail cross-passed their way down the field and McPhail's final touch was a neatly executed chip that left Brown completely stranded.' He converted another couple in the quarters to dump the Dons 3–0, and contributed greatly to eliminating Raith Rovers at the penultimate stage. And in the final, 'McPhail beat Paton to the jump, glided the ball past him, evaded the challenge of Shaw, and forced Johnstone out before lofting the shot over the diving goalkeeper.' He played at centre forward in the 1955 Scottish Cup final, and moved to inside left for the replay, which Celtic lost 1–0 to Clyde. Mc 'Never' Phail retired in 1956 just as his brother Billy signed from Shawfield.

A sports journalist for many years with the *Daily Record* and the *Celtic View*, John McPhail died on 8 November 2000, aged seventy-six.

# Jimmy McStay
Centre half 1921-1934

|  | Appearances | Goals |
| --- | --- | --- |
| League | 409 | 7 |
| Scottish Cup | 63 | 2 |
| Glasgow Cup | 29 | 0 |
| Charity Cup | 18 | 0 |
| Other Competitions | 2 | 0 |
| TOTAL | 521 | 9 |

Inspiring captain and dominant pivot Jimmy McStay followed his brother Willie's coat-tails to Parkhead in 1921. He had previously played for Netherburn Juniors and Larkhall Thistle and made his League debut for Celtic against Clyde on 4 November 1922.

Supporters originally believed that the only reason for his inclusion in the side was because of the presence of his elder brother, Willie. But the criticism did not do Jimmy justice, as he later proved that his selection was made purely on ability. Indeed, chairman Bob Kelly reflected on his career thus: 'There have been few centre-halves who were so adept as Jimmy McStay at heading the ball to one or other of his wing-halves and thereby starting attacks. He was a firm and fair tackler and as captain he set a magnificent example in his dedication to helping Celtic to succeed.'

Although never chosen to represent Scotland in an international match, he did appear three times for the Scottish League. In September 1934, after making well over 450 senior appearances for Celtic, he joined Hamilton Academicals on a free transfer and added backbone to help them reach the Scottish Cup final at the end of that season.

He later managed the Irish club Brideville and was then boss at Alloa Athletic before taking charge at Parkhead for the difficult wartime years. In July 1945, after returning from a family holiday in Ayr, McStay was called to a meeting with chairman Tom White. But even as he stepped off a tram near Parkhead, he caught sight of a newspaper placard announcing his impending dismissal, and that Jimmy McGrory was the likely candidate to take over. The meeting was short, with White asking for his resignation, but it says a great deal for Jimmy McStay's loyalty that he soon offered his services to McGrory as a scout, an offer which the new boss gratefully accepted.

# Paul McStay
Midfielder 1982-1997

| | Appearances | Goals |
|---|---|---|
| League | 509 (6) | 57 |
| Scottish Cup | 66 | 6 |
| League Cup | 54 | 7 |
| Europe | 43 | 2 |
| Other Competitions | 5 | 0 |
| TOTAL | 677 (6) | 72 |

Scottish schoolboy internationalist Paul McStay first came to the public's attention with a wonderful display against England Schoolboys at Wembley in 1980. The Scots won 5–4 and brilliant McStay bagged a brace to help destroy the 'Auld Enemy' in front of a large armchair audience. He capped an exceptional performance away to Aberdeen with a goal in a 3–1 win on 30 January 1982, only a week after making his home debut against Queen of the South in the Scottish Cup. Paul came through the ranks and represented Scotland at every level and won 72 full international caps, playing in the 1986 and 1990 World Cup finals. 'The Maestro' orchestrated Celtic's midfield with an artistic flair and extraordinary vision, but many feel he never really fulfilled his maximum potential. After an excellent 1982/83 campaign, McStay's perfectly weighted passes and rasping shots were major factors behind Celtic winning the double in the club's centenary season, and also helped him collect both the Scottish Football Writers' and Players' Player of the Year awards in 1988.

One of Celtic's finest-ever servants, he took over the club captaincy when Roy Aitken departed for Newcastle United in January 1990, but no matter how hard he tried he never seemed to show the leadership qualities that his predecessor possessed. There was much talk of him leaving Parkhead in the summer of 1992, but the faithful fans were relieved when he committed himself to Celtic for the remainder of his playing days. The 1994/95 season was one of personal despair and joy; first came the anguish of a penalty shoot-out defeat in the Coca-Cola Cup final at the hands of First Division Raith Rovers at Ibrox, when the 'Maestro' missed the all important spot kick, and then came the relief of a long-overdue Scottish Cup final win against Airdrieonians. Paul McStay channelled everything into his game, and if perhaps he lacked that touch of arrogance and selfishness which all star players need, he was nevertheless a truly great Celt. He retired during the closed season of 1997 through injury.

# Willie McStay
Right-back 1912-1929

| | Appearances | Goals |
|---|---|---|
| League | 399 | 37 |
| Scottish Cup | 48 | 3 |
| Glasgow Cup | 25 | 1 |
| Charity Cup | 17 | 3 |
| Other Competitions | 8 | 0 |
| TOTAL | 497 | 44 |

The first of the McStay clan to play for Celtic, sturdy full-back Willie McStay was immediately loaned out to Ayr United for experience after joining the club from Larkhall Thistle in 1912. He was not recalled to Paradise until 1916, having also assisted Belfast Celtic during the early days of the First World War. When he eventually made his League debut for Celtic, it came in a comfortable 5–1 victory over St Mirren at Love Street on 19 August 1916, at the beginning of a season which saw Celts lift the League Championship for a fourth consecutive campaign. A powerful footballer, McStay starred in all the defensive positions, being described as 'strong, steady, robust and totally fearless'. A measure of his build and strength can be gained from his nickname of 'The Tank'. The team's regular penalty-taker, Willie won numerous honours in a career which spanned two decades, including being capped thirteen times for Scotland and playing in ten games for the Scottish League. McStay had a brief spell in American soccer during the summer of 1923 with New York Giants, and was suspended by Celtic on his return to Scotland.

Transferred to Hearts in August 1929, he finished his professional career with the Tynecastle club in the autumn of 1930. Succeeded as Celtic captain by his younger brother, Jimmy, he pulled the hooped jersey over his head for the last time on 27 April 1929, in a 3–2 win at Kilmarnock. A return to Northern Ireland in 1932 saw him manage Glentoran, and he held the same post at Coleraine around 1934. Celtic great Willie McStay died on 3 September 1960.

# Willie Maley
Half-back 1888-1897

| | Appearances | Goals |
|---|---|---|
| League | 75 | 2 |
| Scottish Cup | 26 | 3 |
| Glasgow Cup | 26 | 0 |
| Charity Cup | 9 | 0 |
| Other Competitions | 8 | 1 |
| TOTAL | 144 | 6 |

Celtic's first and longest-serving manager was also a more-than-decent footballer for the club during its infant years. Along with brother Tom he played in the Bhoys' inaugural match on 28 May 1888 and dedicated himself to the cause for the next fifty-two years of his life. Big and strong, Willie Maley had the perfect physique to occupy the half-back berth and with hefty thighs that pumped him over the ground at remarkable speed, he was deemed good enough to represent Scotland against Ireland and England in 1893. Previous to those fixtures he had starred in the Scots' unofficial games against Canada in 1888 and 1891, and further international honours would include two appearances for the Scottish League. Contemporary John McCartney of Rangers and Cowlairs described him thus: 'a stylish as well as a class right half-back. Never flurried and scrupulously fair at all times.' Maley's employers (Messrs Smith & Wilson, Chartered Accountants) once requested him to give up professional football, but Willie continued to play and used his mother's maiden name, Montgomery, to disguise his identity.

A keen sprinter with Clydesdale Harriers, he won the 100-yards championship of Scotland in 1896, a distinction he shares with Olympic heroes Eric Liddell and Allan Wells. After many years as a committee member of the Scottish Amateur Athletics Association, he was elected the organisation's president. As a player with Celtic he took on the added responsibility of match secretary in 1894 and on retirement in 1897 became the club's secretary-manager – a post he held until 1940.

President of the Scottish Football League from 1921 to 1924, outside of the sport, Maley was an astute businessman and a devout and frequent pilgrim to Lourdes. He owned 'The Bank' restaurant in Queen Street, a premises which only recently changed its name to 'Black'. Maley reflected on his exile from Paradise in the following terms: 'Personally I can never forget the 1939/40 season. It has been to me the end of my football career and has robbed me of the very tang of life'. Willie Maley died on 2 April 1958, in the Bon Secours Nursing Home, aged eighty-nine.

# Johnny Madden
Centre forward 1889-1897

| | Appearances | Goals |
|---|---|---|
| League | 92 | 38 |
| Scottish Cup | 25 | 17 |
| Glasgow Cup | 31 | 17 |
| Charity Cup | 16 | 4 |
| Other Competitions | 9 | 5 |
| TOTAL | 173 | 81 |

Shipyard riveter Johnny Madden starred for Dumbarton and joined the Lincolnshire club Gainsborough Trinity in 1887, shortly after representing the Sons of the Rock in that year's Scottish Cup final against Hibernian. Those were hard times for the professional footballer, especially if he had to supplement his wages from the game. Every Friday night, Madden finished his shift at the shipyard before travelling south on the night express. He reached Gainsborough, or wherever Trinity were playing, on the Saturday morning, took part in the match and then received his 'amateur' money before boarding a northbound train to arrive home some time on Sunday and be at work again on Monday morning.

In 1889, he returned to Celtic, having previously played in the club's inaugural match against Rangers on 28 May 1888, and went on to win numerous honours as a fast dangerous striker. Madden became the subject of a 'kidnapping' by Sheffield Wednesday, but their attempt to secure his services was thwarted by a local priest who 'spirited' him back to Glasgow after the player had been only two days in the Yorkshire city.

He scored four goals on his international debut for Scotland, an 8–0 victory over Wales in March 1893. He also hit the target in his only other international appearance a couple of years later, against the same opposition.

When Celtic had their experimental artificial lighting around Christmas 1893, the supporters decided to name the rigging 'Madden's Shipyard' after their favourite forward. An extremely valuable Celt in the club's early years, he moved to Dundee and later played some games for Tottenham Hotspur in their 1897/98 Southern League season. His name is legendary in Czechoslovakia, where he was largely instrumental in introducing the Scottish style to his side, Slavia Prague. 'The fact was that the great Scottish captain, Jackie Robertson, who was a close friend despite being a Rangers player, was offered the Job but passed it on to Madden. Jake quickly had his photograph taken wearing a Rangers jersey and the Czechs were happy to accept him at face value.' Regarding the language barrier Madden commented: 'I learnt enough to swear in – and anyhow, it beats boiler-makin' in the yards.' When he died in April 1948, he was buried in the Olsanke cemetary like a hero. Indeed, when the Hapsburgs ruled the Austro-Hungarian Empire, there was a statue of him erected in Prague.

|  | Appearances | Shut-outs |
|---|---|---|
| League | 94 | 22 |
| Scottish Cup | 6 | 3 |
| League Cup | 23 | 4 |
| Glasgow Cup | 6 | 2 |
| Charity Cup | 7 | 3 |
| Other Competitions | 168 | 42 |
| TOTAL | 304 | 76 |

Brave and stylish with excellent anticipation and clean handling, goalkeeper Willie Miller played in a poor Celtic side, yet, like Frank Haffey, was selected for Scotland against England. He starred with the boys' club St Rollox United before joining Celtic from Maryhill Harp in May 1942. At the time he was training to be an engineer in the railways, so he worked all day and went along to Parkhead at night. Football reporters of the time went into raptures at his superb displays between the posts. A perfect example comes from Celts' goal-less game against Rangers in the Victory Cup semi-final of 1st June 1946: Thornton hit 'a bullet-like drive that was going away from Miller and making for the top left-hand corner of the net. Miller, almost at the opposite post, rose to it in a manner reminiscent of the great John Thomson and turned the ball over the bar for a corner. Celtic can thank Miller for earning them a replay.'

Willie represented Scotland on six occasions, most notably being presented to Prime Minister, Clement Attlee, before the kick-off of the England international at Wembley in 1947. The match ended 1–1, after Miller denied Carter in the dying minutes. He also made a further seven appearances for the Scottish League.

Eventually, however, Miller's form declined and one slip too many led to his departure. On 1 August 1950, he was transferred to Clyde and helped that outfit gain a remarkable haul of silverware during the 1951/52 season – Glasgow Cup, Charity Cup, Supplementary Cup and the Second Division Championship trophy. Miller moved to Hibernian in January 1954, but there he failed to oust Tommy Younger from his guard and retired in the closed season of 1955. He subseqently had a spell as a representative for a whisky firm and also ran a pub in the Townhead area of Glasgow. Despite Celtic's dismal record during his time at Parkhead, he remains one of the club's finest custodians.

Willie Miller died aged eighty in Gartnavel Hospital on 19 June 2005.

# Neil Mochan

Forward 1953-1960

| | Appearances | Goals |
|---|---|---|
| League | 191 | 81 |
| Scottish Cup | 34 | 16 |
| League Cup | 43 | 13 |
| Glasgow Cup | 15 | 4 |
| Charity Cup | 11 | 6 |
| Other Competitions | 4 | 2 |
| TOTAL | 298 | 122 |

Strong, determined forward Neilly Mochan packed a powerful shot in his left foot. Forever remembered in the annals of Celtic FC for his unstoppable screamer in the 1953 Coronation Cup final triumph over Hibs, Mochan was an instant success in Paradise. On his debut, in May 1953, he netted twice in the Charity Cup final victory against Queen's Park at Hampden.

Born in Larbert, Stirlingshire, on 6 April 1927, he signed for Greenock Morton from Dunipace Thistle in 1944 on the recommendation of the great Billy Steel, and stayed with the Cappielow club throughout the 1940s – although National Service prevented him from playing in Morton's epic Scottish Cup final and replay with Rangers in 1948. In May 1951, Mochan moved to Middlesbrough for an amazing £14,000 and scored 14 goals in 38 League appearances for

Boro before Celtic paid £8,000 for him in the spring of 1953. He was the leading League scorer with 20 goals in the double-winning season of 1953/54, and he converted four on the Bhoys' Scottish Cup trail which culminated in a 2–1 defeat of Aberdeen.

Nicknamed 'Smiler', Neil collected three full caps for Scotland and also played in a 'B' international against England in 1954. Towards the end of his Celtic days he took up the left-back berth with a fair degree of success. Transferred to Dundee United for £1,500, he finished his playing career in 1963/64 with Raith Rovers.

Amongst his scoring feats are a brace in Celts' 7–1 hammering of Rangers in the League Cup final of 1957/58, and netting all five goals in a Scottish Cup tie against St Mirren on 29 February 1960. He returned to Parkhead as asssistant trainer/coach in 1964 and became head trainer in the summer of 1965. 'Smiler' sadly died of leukaemia in Falkirk on 28 August 1994. His brother, Denis, played for East Fife, Raith Rovers, Nottingham Forest and Colchester United. A great club man.

# Lubomir Moravcik
### Forward 1998-2002

| | Appearances | Goals |
|---|---|---|
| League | 75 (19) | 29 |
| Scottish Cup | 9 (1) | 1 |
| League Cup | 8 (2) | 2 |
| Europe | 11 (4) | 3 |
| Other Competitions | 0 | 0 |
| TOTAL | 103 (26) | 35 |

The wee man of magic Lubomir Moravcik came to Celtic late in life at the age of thirty-three, but with his sublime skills and marvellous technical touches on the ball he instantly endeared himself to everyone connected with the club. Born in Nitra, Slovakia, on 22 June 1965, Moravcik began his senior career with the little-known Czechoslovakian side Plastika Nitra. He made his name during the Czechs' 1990 World Cup qualifying campaign as an attacking left-sided midfielder who displayed intricate dribbling skills and a powerful shot. One of the few to break the Sparta-Ostrava monopoly of the national team at that time, he proved to be one of the best players on view at Italia '90, although he was ordered off during the quarter-final against West Germany. Lubo's absurd expulsion came about for kicking his boot up in the air after it had come off in a tackle.

He signed for St Etienne that same summer and Les Verts' fans took him to their hearts and compared him with the brilliant Platini. Voted the best foreign footballer in France's First Division, he also won Czechoslovakia's Player of the Year award in 1992. Subsequently with Bastia and the German side MSV Duisburg,

he joined Celtic for £300,000 on 30 October 1998. Two magnificent goals in his first Old Firm encounter in November led Celtic to a 5–1 thrashing of their ancient rivals, but an injury at Motherwell in February robbed the team of his influential presence.

In full flow Moravcik was an absolute delight to watch, and his two solo goals in Celts' 3–0 triumph at Ibrox on 29 April 2001 will long live in the memory. Lubo bowed out of Paradise during the 1–1 draw with Rangers in April 2002, but only after receiving the adulation of a standing ovation from an adoring public. A natural footballer, his testimonial in Slovakia attracted an attendance of 10,000 – five times the average crowd – and raised £5,000 for handicapped children in his home-town of Nitra. Subsequently reunited with Josef Venglos at JEF Ichihara in Japan, and recently named Director of Football at SCP Ruzomberok of Slovakia.

# Bobby Murdoch

Right-half 1959-1973

| | Appearances | Goals |
|---|---|---|
| League | 287 (4) | 61 |
| Scottish Cup | 53 | 13 |
| League Cup | 84 | 17 |
| Europe | 54 | 11 |
| Other Competitions | 25 | 8 |
| TOTAL | 503 (4) | 110 |

'My complete footballer', said Inter Milan coach Helenio Herrera of Bobby Murdoch after the Lisbon Lions' victory in the 1967 European Cup final. 'Murdy' was a forceful, yet beautifully balanced, sophisticated player who laid on a constant stream of inch-perfect, long, probing, defence-splitting passes for his forwards, Jimmy Johnstone being the main recipient.

At Our Lady's High School, Motherwell, Bobby admired the older pupil Billy McNeill and followed him to Celtic Park in August 1959 on provisional forms. Farmed out to Cambuslang Rangers to gain some experience, he trained for two nights a week and during the day was an apprentice sheet-metal worker under the Celtic goalkeeper Frank Connor in Rutherglen – at the same time as Michael Martin, now Speaker of the House of Commons.

He signed permanently in 1961, originally as an inside right, but moved to right-half after Jock Stein took over as Celtic manager in 1965. He was part of the engine room of the team, or as Bertie Auld liked to call himself and Bobby, 'McKellar & Watt' – the link men. Murdoch was

without a doubt one of the most influential post-war Scottish midfielders. In 1969, he received the Scottish Football Writers' Player of the Year award, and the following season he topped a wonderful performance in the European Cup semi-final at Hampden by scoring Celts' winner against Leeds United. Boca Juniors and Everton were amongst a host of teams that came calling for his signature, and in September 1973 he went to Middlesbrough and immediately led the side to the Second Division Championship as well as the Anglo-Scottish Trophy in 1976. He had an unsuccessful stint as manager of the Cleveland club in 1981/82, but it's as a world-class right-half that he will always be remembered and greatly admired throughout football.

Here are just a few of the tributes bestowed upon him by his fellow professionals. Roberto Passaola, coach of Fiorentina, commented: 'Murdoch is the Papa of the team; the rest are the sons around him.' Graeme Souness recalled: 'He came along at just the right time, not only for me but the whole team – Middlesbrough. His experience settled us down as we went for pro-motion and he also proved to be a big influence on my career. Bobby was a great passer of the ball and he had an excellent attitude. He would always pull me to one side to pass on advice or tell me when he thought I was acting wrongly.' Jack Charlton said: 'I have never in my life seen

A young Bobby Murdoch serves his apprenticeship as a sheet-metal worker and shares a joke with Frank Connor.

a better passer of the ball than Bobby Murdoch. I mean, when he hit them, the ball appeared to hold up in the air, or alternatively gather speed to find the player running on to it, in precisely the right stride. It was, of course, an optical illusion, but that was the measure of the man's timing.'

He had a weight problem, which Jock Stein tried to address by sending him to a health farm for two weeks. 'First week, I lost about 15lb', Murdoch said. 'The second week, I put it all on again.' Perhaps the main reason behind his condition was a persistent ankle injury, which precluded hard training. When he was sent to play in the reserves at East Fife in October 1972, Ian Archer described it like 'asking Andre Previn to conduct the London Symphony Orchestra in the middle of Central Station on Friday of Fair Week.'

In 1995, he made legal history when the Medical Appeal Tribunal ruled that his ankle injury, from a match in 1962, was an industrial accident, which meant he could claim back-dated disability benefit. His health deteriorated in his final years, and he died after a stroke on 15 May 2001, aged fifty-six. When a foreign journalist was asked to sum up the Celtic team of the Lisbon era, he smiled, shrugged and replied in one word – 'Mur-dock'. It is appropriate that the last word should go to his mentor Jock Stein: 'As far as I am concerned, Murdoch was just about the best player I had as manager. I only let him move because he had run out of challenges with Celtic.'

101

# Frank Murphy
Left-winger 1933-1945

|  | Appearances | Goals |
|---|---|---|
| League | 144 | 46 |
| Scottish Cup | 17 | 4 |
| Glasgow Cup | 7 | 1 |
| Charity Cup | 8 | 3 |
| Other Competitions | 95 | 31 |
| TOTAL | 271 | 85 |

Nippy, light and elusive. Born at Gartcosh on 6 December 1915, Frank Murphy began his playing career in Boys' Guild football at Glenboig and Coatbridge. With devastating pace down the left flank, Frank Murphy was a direct winger who loved to cut inside and have a pop at goal in addition to providing pinpoint crosses for McGrory & Co.

Previously with Croy Celtic, Frank also had a spell with St Roch's for development before returning to Parkhead at the tail end of the 1933/34 season – netting a brace on his debut in a 4–2 win against Airdrieonians on 7 April 1934. He soon solved the left-wing problem that had dogged Celtic since the departure of Adam McLean some years earlier, and became a valuable member of the club's famed inter-changing attack in the late 1930s.

Murphy scored on his international debut with a superb solo effort, in Amsterdam when Scotland defeated Holland 3–1 in May 1938, yet was never again selected to wear the dark blue jersey. However, he did represent the Scottish League in a 5–2 victory over the Irish League at Ibrox on 2 September 1936, when he once again found the target. Murphy converted a creditable ratio of goals (54 in 176 League and domestic cup games – not including wartime matches), and played in two Championship teams, as well as in the 1937 Scottish Cup and 1938 Empire Exhibition Trophy winning sides. He continued to assist the Celts during the early years of the war before moving on loan to Albion Rovers in August 1942 (where a youthful Jock Stein would be one of his team-mates).

Called up for the RAF in February 1943, he spent much of the following year at Aldershot FC. Frank Murphy later became a publican in Coatbridge, and died on 12 February 1984 after a fairly long illness which he bore uncomplainingly.

# Charlie Napier
Left-winger 1929-1935

| | Appearances | Goals |
|---|---|---|
| League | 177 | 82 |
| Scottish Cup | 24 | 13 |
| Glasgow Cup | 11 | 4 |
| Charity Cup | 6 | 3 |
| Other Competitions | 0 | 0 |
| TOTAL | 218 | 102 |

The scintillating attacker Charlie Napier looked set for a very long career with Celtic, but when the club refused his request for a benefit at the end of the 1934/35 season, he asked for a transfer and moved to England. Nicknamed 'Happy Feet' because of his nimble running style and zigzag dribbles, Napier, a two-footed direct forward who possessed a great burst of speed over 25 yards, was the son of a Falkirk FC secretary. A Bainsford boy, Charles Edward Napier junior worked as an electrician before Celtic signed him from Alva Albion Rangers in the autumn of 1928 and loaned him out to the now defunct junior side Maryhill Hibs. He returned to Paradise the next year and made his home debut on 19 October 1929, at outside left in a 2–1 League win over Queen's Park. Besides his pace, Charlie had brilliant ball conrol and a terrific shot.

The delicious cunning of 'Happy Feet' got Celts back into the 1931 Scottish Cup final against Motherwell with a lovely lob over 'Well's wall for the darting McGrory to toe-poke home – the rest is history. He got the first of five international caps for Scotland against England at Wembley on 9 April 1932, and provided the inch-perfect corner-kicks from which Dally Duncan – later to be a team-mate at Derby County – converted to gain a memorable victory over the Auld Enemy at Hampden on 6 April 1935.

That summer, Napier moved to the Baseball Ground for £5,000 and within twelve months had played in every position in the Rams' forward line, earning Derby a rare point at Arsenal when he turned out at centre forward following injuries to Jack Bowers and Hughie Gallacher. Transferred to Sheffield Wednesday in March 1938, Charlie guested for his home-town team, Falkirk, during the last wartime campaign, earlier having been capped in an unofficial international. He ended his career with Stenhousemuir, from September 1946 until he retired in 1948. Charlie 'Happy Feet' Napier won two Scottish Cup winners' medals in 1931 and 1933 and also represented the Scottish League on a couple of occasions. He was apparently a bit of a ladies' man in the 1930s, fifty years before Celts other 'Charlie N'. His brother, George, played in defence for Kilmarnock and Cowdenbeath.

| | Appearances | Goals |
|---|---|---|
| League | 159 (28) | 85 |
| Scottish Cup | 9 (2) | 7 |
| League Cup | 24 (7) | 26 |
| Europe | 16 (4) | 7 |
| Other Competitions | 4 | 2 |
| TOTAL | 212 (41) | 127 |

Charlie Nicholas was from the Wyndford area of Maryhill – he lived next door to fellow Celtic prodigy Jim Duffy. Whereas Duffy had to move to Morton to find first-team football, Charlie Nic' made his debut in a 1–0 home defeat from Ayr United in the Drybrough Cup on 27 July 1980. He attended St Gregory's primary and St Columba of Iona secondary schools, worked as an apprentice mechanic and had trials with Ipswich Town and Wolves before emerging from the talented Celtic Boys' Club in 1979. Nicholas could dribble, pass and shoot to a high standard, and had a fantastic first season in the top team (1980/81) with 28 goals in all competitions – none more pleasing than his single strike against Rangers at Ibrox in April which virtually sealed the Championship's destination.

The boy with the floppy hairstyle and trendy dress sense was just as flamboyant off the field, but soon faced a head on confrontation with manager Billy McNeill, who had a strict policy on dress and appearance. One incident culminated in Charlie being fined for not wearing socks. Like Larsson almost two decades later, he recovered from a broken leg to head the charts in 1982/83 with 48 goals. Danny McGrain later recalled how Charlie became the centre of unwanted attention in a pub from a jealous player with a side from the lower league who lectured him: 'I can do anything you can do, pal, anything!' To which Charlie replied, 'Oh, yeah? Can you do this, then?' Whereupon he took out a £20 note and tore it up in front of the guy's face. However, after the embarrassed punter stormed off, speechless, Charlie was quick to recover his money from the floor and borrow sellotape.

He chose Arsenal over Man United and Liverpool when he signed in the summer of 1983 for £750,000, and immediately became the idol of the North Bank. He scored both the Gunners' goals when they beat Liverpool in the 1987 Littlewoods Cup final at Wembley, but new boss George Graham saw Charlie as surplus to requirements and sold him to Aberdeen for £500,000 in January 1988. His second stint at Parkhead proved an unsuccessful period in the club's history, but he still showed some sublime delicate touches on the ball which delighted the fans. He went to Clyde in 1995 on a free transfer, and retired the following year. Nicholas now provides intelligent comment on live football for Sky Sports.

| | Appearances | Goals |
|---|---|---|
| League | 164 | 17 |
| Scottish Cup | 47 | 7 |
| Glasgow Cup | 24 | 1 |
| Charity Cup | 20 | 1 |
| Other Competitions | 47 | 2 |
| TOTAL | 302 | 28 |

Whether at left-back or left-half, Willie Orr was an 'out-and out footballer blessed with sound judgement', who enjoyed a successful career both as a player and manager. Orr started with Juniors Airdrie Fruitfield FC and then starred for Airdrieonians and Preston North End before joining Celtic in April 1897. He could play in any defensive position 'with ease' and was said to have been the 'inventor' of the pass back. Born in Shotts on 20 June 1873, Orr made his Celtic debut in a Glasgow League match against Rangers on 1 May 1897, and was an original member of the famous 'six-in-a-row' team.

Willie became the first player to score a penalty in a Scottish Cup final, when he converted from the spot in Celtic's 3–0 victory over Hearts in 1907, and retired that same year having amassed four League Championship badges, three Scottish Cup winner's medals, three Scotland caps and a representative appearance for Glasgow against Sheffield, as well as Glasgow and Charity Cup honours.

He was a member of Airdrieonians' board of directors from 1909 until 1921, when he became the club's secretary-manager, a position he held until July 1926, leaving to manage Leicester City. In 1924 he steered the 'Diamonds' to the only Scottish Cup final triumph in their history and guided them to three runners–up places in a row in the old First Division from 1922 to 1925. At Filbert Street he again showed his prowess as a great manager by taking the provincial 'Foxes' to third in Division One in 1927/28 and runners-up to Sheffield Wednesday the following season. He was then boss at Falkirk from June 1932 to April 1935, when he received a suspension (lifted in February 1937) after being found guilty of bribery charges, including offering Ayr United player Robert Russell £3 not to play in a crucial relegation game against Falkirk. Although this episode ended his managerial career, it should not blacken his reputation as a fine footballer who provided Celtic with a decade of dedicated service.

| | Appearances | Goals |
|---|---|---|
| League | 174 | 11 |
| Scottish Cup | 20 | 1 |
| Glasgow Cup | 10 | 0 |
| Charity Cup | 11 | 0 |
| Other Competitions | 115 | 5 |
| TOTAL | 330 | 17 |

One of Celtic's finest-ever left-halves, George Paterson was a solid, dependable, hard-working player whose main asset was his awesome passing ability. Indeed, such clean, neat and intelligent distribution of the ball got him an international call up in the autumn of 1938 – a 2–0 win against Ireland in Belfast on 8 October with club-mate Jimmy Delaney scoring for the Scots.

Like 'Wembley Wizard' Jimmy McMullen, George was Denny born and bred and joined Celtic from Dunipace Juniors in March 1932. Playing at centre forward – for McGrory, who had injured himself in the Scottish Cup final a few days earlier – Paterson scored on his debut in a 2–1 win over Airdrieonians at Parkhead on 18 April 1933.

He served in the RAF during the war and, like many other players, turned out as a guest for several teams including Leicester City, Blackpool, and Wolves, and as a result made only sporadic appearances for Celtic throughout the conflict. However, on one such occasion he netted the goal that settled the Ne'erday 1945 game at Ibrox against Rangers with a stunning 30-yard drive. In October 1946, he moved to Brentford while serving a suspension imposed by the SFA (a result of the Victory Cup farce, when the skipper Paterson was sent off after refusing to hand over the ball when the referee, who some players claimed smelt of alcohol, awarded Rangers a penalty).

The London outfit were then in the old First Division, and George went to Griffin Park in a straight exchange for veteran striker Jerry McAloon. Paterson played in 62 League games for Brentford before switching to the Southern League with Yeovil in October 1949. Appointed manager of Stirling Albion in October 1951, he resigned the following summer after a dressing-room bust-up. Celtic's coach from 1953 to 1956, he emigrated to New Zealand in 1985 where he died in late December of that year, aged seventy-one.

# Bertie Peacock
Left-half 1949-1961

| | Appearances | Goals |
|---|---|---|
| League | 318 | 32 |
| Scottish Cup | 56 | 8 |
| League Cup | 80 | 10 |
| Glasgow Cup | 24 | 6 |
| Charity Cup | 18 | 2 |
| Other Competitions | 10 | 2 |
| TOTAL | 506 | 60 |

Captain of Celtic in the famous 7–1 victory over Rangers in the 1957/58 League Cup final, and known as the 'Little Ant' during the 1958 World Cup finals in Sweden, Bertie Peacock converted from being a skilful creative inside forward to a more purposeful role as an industrious tenacious left-half. He soon established a perfect understanding down the left with fellow Irishman Sean Fallon, and formed part of the marvellous half-back line of Evans, Stein and Peacock which was the foundation of Celts' double triumph of 1953/54.

Coleraine-born Bertie joined Celtic in 1949 from Glentoran, having previously played for his home-town team. In his *Coleraine FC: A History*, published in 1988, Grant Cameron tells how Peacock went to Glasgow by boat and arrived at 6.30 a.m., clutching a piece of paper which carried the name and address of his landlady. 'I was just a young lad lost in the big city,' recalled Peacock. 'I walked around for two hours and finally summed up enough courage to ask for directions from someone. They put me on a tramcar. When I finally got to the tenement block, I stood in the hallway reading the occupants' names, looking for my landlady. A door opened and an elderly woman asked me who I was looking for. When I explained, she told me the woman had been taken ill and rushed into hospital two days earlier. If I had anyone

to take me home there and then, I would have gone back,' he admitted. Eventually, Peacock found his way to Parkhead. He said: 'I walked about for ages before I found the street which led to the main entrance. You should have seen me wandering around. I'm sure I looked bewildered.' In the hallway Peacock walked straight into the manager, who told him to go and train. There was nobody else in the stadium except one man running around the perimeter track. He asked the youngster if he wanted to run with him and Peacock remembers not being able to keep pace with him. 'I later discovered he was the great Tommy Docherty,' he said.

On 31 August 1949 Bertie made his debut in a 1–3 League Cup reverse at the hands of Aberdeen. However, his Scottish League debut

The Celtic double-winning team of 1953/54 with Bertie Peacock positioned far right, back row.

did not come until 3 January, at Raith Rovers, and for most of his initial twelve months at Parkhead he played in the Reserves. The end of that first season, though, did provide a memorable moment for the young Ulsterman, when he gained a winner's medal after Celtic defeated Rangers 3–2 to take the Charity Cup.

The following term, Peacock established himself and throughout the next decade he missed very few games. Although not a flamboyant player, he proved an important figure in the club's successes of the 1950s. A member of the Great Britain side which met the Rest of Europe in the Irish FA's seventy-fifth anniversary and always a fanatical trainer, Bertie returned to Ireland to become player-manager of Coleraine in 1961. In October the following year, he succeeded Peter Doherty as Northern Ireland manager, carrying out his national duties in tandem with those at his club. His successful thirteen-year career as Coleraine's boss was crowned by the team's first Irish League Championship in 1974, and in recent times he

has followed in his father's footsteps by becoming a director of Coleraine FC.

He was once a member of the Sports Council for Northern Ireland and has been one of the enthusiastic people in the Coleraine & District Sports Council, which hopes to look after the welfare of individuals and teams in various sports in the borough. A one time delicatessen owner and publican, on a visit to Glasgow for Celtic's Centenary celebrations, he said: 'I still retain a great affection for Celtic and the time I was associated with them. They were good times and although we had our disappointments, the overall reflection was of a happy club. Now and then it could be hard, but in general it was a happy experience. On more than one occasion I could have left the club and accepted offers from England, but nothing could outweigh the pride I had playing for Celtic. That was all that mattered.' Capped on 31 occasions for Northern Ireland, and awarded the MBE for his services to soccer in 1986. This truly great celt died in late July 2004, aged seventy-five.

# Davie Provan

Outside right 1978-1986

| | Appearances | Goals |
|---|---|---|
| League | 192 (14) | 28 |
| Scottish Cup | 29 | 2 |
| League Cup | 41 (1) | 11 |
| Europe | 25 (1) | 1 |
| Other Competitions | 9 | 1 |
| TOTAL | 296 (16) | 43 |

An elusive forward who bewildered defences with his wing play, Davie Provan had an exceptional ability at bending in pin-point curving centres which brought numerous goals for Celtic. Born in Gourock, Renfrewshire, on 8 May 1956, Provan began his career with local junior side Port Glasgow and signed for Kilmarnock in 1974. He cost Celtic £125,000 (a then record transfer fee between Scottish clubs) from the Rugby Park outfit on 18 September 1978.

An entertainer who also excelled at the taking of free-kicks and corners, Provan won the Scottish Players' Player of the Year award in 1980, a wonderful tribute to his skilful approach. Supremely confident, during an Old Firm game, he told Rangers' Alex MacDonald that he could 'keep a beach-ball off him in a telephone box'. It was Davie's wonderfully flighted free-kick to the postage stamp position that got Celtic back into the 1985 Scottish Cup final against Dundee United.

Alas, late in 1985, just when he was playing the best football of his career, Davie fell victim to a viral illness and although he made one appearance thereafter, the disease robbed him of much-needed energy and cut short his career. On 30 November 1987, Celtic honoured him with a testimonial match against Nottingham Forest, a game that saw Kenny Dalglish make a guest appearance in the hoops. Davie Provan retired, looking back on a playing career which saw him collect ten full caps for Scotland and play once each for the under-23 side and the Scottish League. Having gathered four Championship, two Scottish Cup and one League Cup winner's medals, he remained on the groundstaff, helping Jimmy Johnstone with coaching the youngsters. Today he gives his opinion on football on Sky Sports, Radio Clyde and in the *Daily Express*.

| | Appearances | Goals |
|---|---|---|
| League | 271 | 191 |
| Scottish Cup | 58 | 30 |
| Glasgow Cup | 39 | 22 |
| Charity Cup | 21 | 14 |
| Other Competitions | 35 | 11 |
| TOTAL | 424 | 268 |

Physical forward Jimmy Quinn 'gave no quarter and asked for none'; 'he used muscular shoulders when dribbling and exploited a shattering left foot shot'. A reluctant recruit to the Celtic cause, the *Croy Express* felt that he should remain a junior player with Smithston Albion and continue to work down the pit, rather than sign professionally for the Bhoys. Thankfully, 'Maley persisted and coaxed the youngster to sign a registration form, promising not to send it to the SFA without Quinn's permission.' An invitation and friendly welcome to a training session at Rothesay in January 1901 persuaded him otherwise, and after a stumbling start, Jimmy soon set the heather on fire with his powerful charges, rampaging runs and fierce shooting.

Adored by the supporters and an inspirational figure in Celts' forward line, Quinn first came to prominence by scoring three times to defeat Rangers 3–2 in the British League Cup final of 1902 at Cathkin Park. Another hat-trick in the 1904 Scottish Cup final again against Rangers gave him legendary status amongst the Legions. To them he could do no wrong, and when controversy raged over a sending-off and suspension by the SFA after an alleged assault on Alec Craig of Rangers in the following season's Scottish Cup semi-final, they raised an astronomical £277 16s 1d on his behalf. Indeed, his 'victim' Craig and his mother both gave evidence for Quinn in court to clear his name from damning press reports of violent conduct. Equally, Willie Maley, always an apologist for his swashbuckling leader, suggested that Quinn's indiscretions were exaggerated: 'All the men that Quinn killed are still alive.' The 'big brother' of Celts' wonderful forward line of Bennett, McMenemy, Quinn, Somers and Hamilton, he would protect and perhaps even seek revenge if any of his smaller colleagues were ill-treated.

After the record-breaking six-in-a-row Championship success (1904–10), one respected reporter wrote:'There are few more earnest players in Scotland than the Celtic centre forward Jimmy Quinn. He has been the potent force, controlling pivot, in establishing this record. His escapement from injury has been phenomenal. His gritty, cast-iron and determined build have so persistently worked towards the objectives

Caricature of the 'Mighty' Jimmy Quinn.

of the team.' When Jimmy made the first goal and scored the second in Scotland's 2–0 win over England at Hampden Park in 1910, the *Daily Mail* observed: 'In Quinn they [Scotland] have undoubtedly the finest centre in the four countries – strong, resolute, and dashing, sometimes opening the game up for his wings and on other occasions going right through himself, but nearly always doing the best thing possible under the circumstances.'

Dogged and damaged in almost every game he played, the 'man of a hundred injuries' appropriately endorsed products like 'Boag's Rheumatic Rum'. He also agreed to have his name associated with some newspaper articles, but after his face appeared on hoardings all over Glasgow, he wanted to cancel the contract and had to be dissuaded from ripping up the cheque he had already accepted.

He retired after a 1–1 draw against Hearts at Parkhead on 30 January 1915, having missed almost all of the previous 1913/14 season through persistent knee trouble. The modest clay-pipe smoking gentleman from Croy died on 20 November 1945, and Willie Maley eloquently summed up his contribution as 'the keystone in the greatest team the Celtic ever had'. His son, James junior, starred at outside left for Cumbernauld Thistle in the 1930s, whilst his grandson, James III, played for Celtic around 1970.

# Peter Scarff

Inside left 1928-1933

|  | Appearances | Goals |
| --- | --- | --- |
| League | 97 | 51 |
| Scottish Cup | 15 | 4 |
| Glasgow Cup | 9 | 5 |
| Charity Cup | 7 | 3 |
| Other Competitions | 0 | 0 |
| TOTAL | 128 | 63 |

Peter Scarff was a powerful inside forward and fine marksman with excellent positional sense, but his career was tragically ended by an illness which eventually proved fatal. Born at Linwood on 29 March 1908, after a brief spell with Maryhill Hibs he made his Celtic debut in a 5–1 home win over Arthurlie in the Scottish Cup on 19 January 1929. Scarff could not only get past opponents, but also put the ball away on a regular basis. Indeed, he netted ten goals from four consecutive league games during the February/March period of 1930. Such consistency caught the attention of the international selectors and Peter duly received a full cap in a goal-less match against Ireland on 21 February 1931. He starred in Celts' Glasgow Cup and Scottish Cup-winning sides of the 1930/31

season, but before the year was out he had sadly played in his last football match.

Eugene MacBride's monumental tome *An Alphabet of The Celts* tells of the decline in his health which led to his early death. 'He watched with concern as John Thomson was carried off to die at Ibrox on 5 September 1931. Eighteen days later, in Willie Fleming's benefit at Ayr, he was unable to resume for the second half and Denis Currie went on in his place. His last game for Celtic was at left-half versus Leith at Parkhead (19 December 1931), and on 12 January 1932 he was admitted to the Bridge of Weir sanatorium seriously ill with pulmonary tuberculosis. Despite periods of remissions giving rise to false hope, it was announced on 29 July 1933 that Peter Scarff would never play football again.' He died on 9 December 1933, aged only twenty-five, and was buried at the beautiful Kilbarchan Cemetery three days later. Willie Maley laid a Celtic jersey on the coffin before the interment.

| | Appearances | Shut-outs |
|---|---|---|
| League | 421 | 224 |
| Scottish Cup | 23 | 13 |
| Glasgow Cup | 25 | 8 |
| Charity Cup | 23 | 11 |
| Other Competitions | 11 | 3 |
| TOTAL | 503 | 259 |

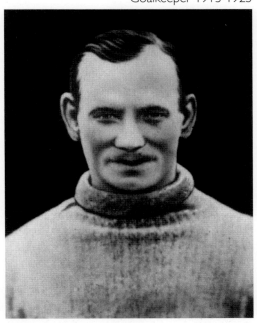

'Oh Charlie Shaw! He never saw / Where Alan Morton pit the ba' / He put the ba' right in the net / And Charlie Shaw sat doon and gret.' That was the verse from Rangers fans after the 'Wee Blue Devil' scored a marvellous goal against Celtic at Parkhead. The memory of Morton's strike past such a great goalkeeper was cherished by Ibrox followers and the tale gained a place in Scottish football folklore.

Born at Twechar on 21 September 1885, Shaw made his name with Queen's Park Rangers and had previously played for Bailleston Thistle, Kirkintilloch Harp and Port Glasgow Athletic. Similar in style and build to Dan McArthur, on returning to Scotland in May 1913 he took up residence in Lennoxtown and made his debut for Celtic in that year's Charity Cup semi-final tie against Third Lanark, being retained for the final success over Rangers a few days later. In 1913/14, Shaw's first full season at Parkhead, he conceded a mere 14 goals and kept a 'clean sheet' in 26 out of 38 League games – a record which has yet to be broken.

He formed a perfect understanding with full-backs McNair and Dodds – 'the Impenetrable Triangle', yet incredibly Charlie was never capped for Scotland. However, he did represent the Scottish League on two occasions. During an illustrious playing career he also owned a tobacconist's shop and bookstall a short distance from the ground at Bridgeton Cross. After a brief loan period with Clyde, he became player-manager of the US side New Bedford in the summer of 1925, taking several players including his Celtic team-mate Andy McAtee with him. The great Charlie Shaw died of pneumonia in New York City on 27 March 1938.

# Ronnie Simpson
Goalkeeper 1964-1969

|  | Appearances | Shut-outs |
| --- | --- | --- |
| League | 118 | 54 |
| Scottish Cup | 17 | 10 |
| League Cup | 29 | 14 |
| Europe | 23 | 12 |
| Other Competitions | 5 | 5 |
| TOTAL | 192 | 95 |

'Faither' Simpson's career looked as good as over in 1958 because of injury, yet incredibly nine years later he won a European Cup winner's medal, was voted Scottish Player of the Year and became the oldest debutant for Scotland (aged 36 years and 186 days) in the famous 3–2 win at Wembley on 15 April 1967.

The son of Jimmy Simpson of Rangers and Scotland fame, Ronnie made his debut for Queens Park at the tender age of 14 years and 234 days. The youngster was still attending King's Park School when he was summoned to the headmaster's room, for what he thought would be a ticking-off about poor exam results. Waiting for him, though, was a delegation from Queen's Park, who wanted him to play against Clyde in the Summer Cup because Scottish international Bobby Brown could not get leave from military service.

He cost Newcastle United £8,750 from Third Lanark in February 1951 and, having already played in the 1948 Olympics for Great Britain under the tutorship of Matt Busby, he went on to win FA Cup medals with Newcastle in 1952 and 1955. After seven years at St James's Park, Simpson was badly injured whilst on the Magpies' trip to Romania in 1958 and was out of the game for almost two years. He fought back to fitness and in October 1960 moved to Hibernian for £2,000, but when Jock Stein took over at Easter Road he left for the same sum to Celtic in September 1964.

Ironically, the 'Big Man' who sold him relighted his career at Parkhead after both buried their differences. Simpson is perhaps best remembered for his back-heel outside the penalty area in Lisbon, but unfortunately a recurrence of a shoulder injury against Ayr United in the 1969/70 League Cup semi-final at Hampden ultimately ended his playing days.

He then acted as coach/scout for Celtic before becoming manager of Hamilton Accies during the 1971/72 season. Subsequently he ran a sports shop in Edinburgh, and also served as a Conservative councillor in the capital. In later life a goalkeeping coach at Dunfermline Athletic and a member of the Pools Panel, Ronnie Simpson died on 20 April 2004, aged seventy-three.

| | Appearances | Goals |
|---|---|---|
| League | 185 | 56 |
| Scottish Cup | 33 | 12 |
| Glasgow Cup | 27 | 11 |
| Charity Cup | 14 | 4 |
| Other Competitions | 31 | 9 |
| TOTAL | 290 | 92 |

An exceptionally fine old-fashioned inside forward with clever footwork, Peter Somers supplied his partners with a constant stream of inch-perfect passes which resulted in many goals for Celtic. He began his playing career at Hamilton Athletic before joining Celtic from the quaintly named Cadzow Oak during the 1897/98 season. Rather surprisingly, Celtic transferred him 'on loan' to Blackburn Rovers in February 1900 for £200 and he scored 13 goals in seventy-eight outings for them before returning to Paradise in 1902, for £120. Blackburn wanted to keep him and offered Celtic a bigger fee, but Willie Maley pressed for his return.

A colourful character, Somers was a past master in the art of repartee. When Fitchie of Queen's Park went in with a high tackle on Peter, Somers shouted over to the 'Spider', 'Play the game!' Fitchie ran after him: 'How should I play the game?' 'Quick as a flash,' Peter replied. 'Just watch me.' While playing against Third Lanark one day, Peter, in a pause during the game, found himself being stared at by the Warriors' big and burly centre half. 'Whit are you looking at me like that for?' asked Peter meekly. 'Huh,' said the Warrior. 'I never saw legs sa sma' as yours. I was wonderin' whaur ye got them.' 'Oh,' replied Peter patly, 'Ma legs. I got them frae ma mither and faither on ma first birthday.' Once he received a letter from a young admirer who wrote with a plea for help: 'Will you please give me your advice, seeing I've now got my place in the school team. I play where you play, at inside left, and I want you to tell me the easiest way to get round a back.' Somers duly obliged. He wrote this simple four word reply: 'Go through a close.'

A key member of Celtic's six-in-a-row side, he won four full caps for Scotland, making his debut in a 4–0 win over Ireland on 18 March 1905. He also represented the Scottish League on three occasions.

He retired in 1910 and subsequently became a director of Hamilton Academicals, and set himself up with a small business in the town. However – sad to relate – he contracted a chill in November 1914 and, with leg trouble setting in, it was necessary to amputate part of his left leg. Two weeks later he passed away in a Glasgow nursing home aged only thirty-six, leaving behind a wife and young family. It was a tragic end to a life filled with joy.

The following week's *Glasgow Observer* said of him: 'Readers of this column are not required to

The great Celtic squad of 1906/07. Peter Somers is third from the left, front row.

be told much of the late Peter Somers, as a player or a pal. He was what I might term the public property of the Celtic club, and its supporters from Camlachie to California. His inimitable touches on the field and witty sayings in the pavilion were known to all at first hand or by reputation, and all the time he was the perfect gentleman, never saying or doing anything to cause a moment's resentment. Thus what player could resist the flash of wit revealed by the reply to one of his own side when that comrade was asked to pass the ball more frequently to the left wing, saying: "Don't talk to me." Back came the answer from Peter: "Well can I write to you?" Playing football, solo whist, or the piano, he was out to enjoy himself and make everybody happy and I need not add he was always successful, for there was no resisting the Mark Tapley of Parkhead, one who looked on the bright side of things. [...] Like Barrie's Peter, he refused to grow up, in seriousness: to the last he was just an overgrown, laughing boy, unable to say an unkind word, because it was not in his nature to be unkind or ungenerous.'

# Jock Stein
## Centre half 1951-1956

| | Appearances | Goals |
|---|---|---|
| League | 106 | 2 |
| Scottish Cup | 21 | 0 |
| League Cup | 20 | 0 |
| Glasgow Cup | 8 | 0 |
| Charity Cup | 6 | 0 |
| Other Competitions | 3 | 0 |
| TOTAL | 164 | 2 |

At his own admittance Jock Stein was only an average footballer, but in a team game greatness comes through in different guises. The 'Big Man's' case for a place in Celtic's Hall of Fame as a player lies in the argument that the Bhoys would not have won the Coronation Cup in 1953 and the League and Cup double the following year had it not been for Stein's organisational skills. Bertie Peacock underlined this assertion on Jock's death in 1985, by recalling that they would meet up at Ferrera's restaurant along with a few other team-mates and go through tactics using the salt and pepper pots as players.

A Lanarkshire man from the Rangers stronghold of Burnbank, Stein used his strength of character to overcome the bigotry when he joined Celtic in December 1951 from Welsh club Llanelli as a third centre half to bring on the young reserves at Parkhead. Born on 5 October 1922, John Stein was born with a 'lucky cap', an extra flap of skin which the Lanarkhire mining community believed brought good luck. Stein was certainly destined to greatness. His playing career took two unexpected turns which resulted in him leading Celtic to League and cup glory. The young Stein worked down the pit as a Bevan Boy and played centre half as a part-timer for both Blantyre Victoria and Albion Rovers, making over 200 League appearances for the Coatbridge club.

In January 1950, following a dispute with Rovers, he decided on full-time football in Wales with Llanelli Town. He might have stayed in Welsh soccer, but for a break-in at his house in Hamilton which saw him return to Scotland to sort out the mess. That piece of misfortune had a silver lining. Thanks to chief scout Jimmy Gribben, Celtic signed Stein as an experienced player to help develop the youth policy at the club. A second freakish stroke of fortune in his first week at Parkhead saw regular pivots Mallan and Boden both injured and Jock pushed into the side as a stop-gap replacement. He never looked back and proved a natural leader on the football field, being both tactically sound and renowned for his defensive clearances with the knee. An ankle injury sustained in a home League Cup tie against Rangers in August 1955 saw the beginning of the end of his playing career. An attempted rehabilitation failed and he wore the hoops for the last time against Coleraine in a closed-season friendly in 1956.

# Chris Sutton

Centre half/Striker 2000-Present

|  | Appearances | Goals |
|---|---|---|
| League | 120 (2) | 61 |
| Scottish Cup | 16 | 5 |
| League Cup | 7 (1) | 2 |
| Europe | 41 (2) | 16 |
| Other Competitions | 0 | 0 |
| TOTAL | 184 (5) | 84 |

Chris Sutton is arguably the finest alternate centre half/centre forward since the days of the late great John Charles of Wales. Born in Nottingham on 10 March 1973, Christopher Roy Sutton made his league debut for Norwich City as a trainee when he replaced ex-Ranger Robert Fleck during a 1–0 win over QPR on 4 May 1991. He progressed to sign professional forms at Carrow Road on 2 July 1991, and had a distinguished career with the Canaries before joining Kenny Dalglish's Blackburn Rovers for £5 million in the summer of 1994. Sutton's partnership with Alan Shearer at Ewood Park became known as the 'SAS' by the media, and their potent pairing propelled Blackburn Rovers to the Premiership title in 1995. Chris was also deemed good enough by his fellow professionals to be elected for the PFA PL Team

Award that year. Injury dogged him the following term and also in his last season at Blackburn in 1998/99, when he had ankle problems caused by stress fractures, but the big man still commanded the third highest transfer fee between British clubs as Chelsea paid £10 million for him on 5 July 1999.

After a nightmare twelve months at Stamford Bridge, 'Sutty' became Martin O'Neill's first signing when Celtic forked out £6 million in July 2000. A few weeks later he had become a hero figure among the supporters with a brace of goals in the Hoops' 6–2 demolition of Rangers at Parkhead. On 7 December 2002 Sutton claimed the fastest goal in the history of Old Firm games, eighteen seconds after kick-off, and more recently he collected Larsson's flick and dinked the ball over Klos to score an outrageous last-gasp winner at Celtic Park. He is commanding in the air, sound in his positional play and radar-like in his distribution – the long ball to set up Larsson's equaliser in the 2004 Scottish Cup final being a perfect example. These qualities were recognised by his fellow professionals in 2004 with the SPFA Player of the Year award.

# Alec Thomson

Inside forward 1922-1934

| | Appearances | Goals |
|---|---|---|
| League | 391 | 88 |
| Scottish Cup | 59 | 15 |
| Glasgow Cup | 27 | 7 |
| Charity Cup | 18 | 1 |
| Other Competitions | 2 | 0 |
| TOTAL | 497 | 111 |

A bricklayer by trade, Alec Thomson's constructive skills were also in evidence on the football field, where his role was that of 'playmaker'. Buckhaven-born Thomson played with local junior sides Glencraig Celtic and Wellesley before coming to Glasgow in 1922.

He made his senior debut in a 1–0 League victory over Clyde at Shawfield on 4 November 1922 and quickly settled at Parkhead as an inside left, but moved along to the inside right position after the departure of Patsy Gallagher to Falkirk in 1926. Frail and not notably fast, Alec's slight build was outweighed by his remarkable ball control and superb accurate passing, which became Celts' lethal weapon in attack. He emerged as an integral part of the Celtic forward line and helped the club to six Scottish Cup final appearances in the space of nine seasons. However, his only League Championship badge was won after the 1925/26 campaign.

He received five outings for the Scottish League and won the first of three full international caps at Old Trafford against England on 17 April 1926, when Scotland scored a famous victory thanks to a goal from the 'Gay Cavalier', Alec Jackson.

Thomson finished his playing days where they began, in the kingdom of Fife, with the recently promoted Dunfermline Athletic in 1934, just as the 'Pars' moved into the old First Division. Alec scored 98 goals in his aggregate 470 Division One outings. He retired from the game in 1937, and died in 1975.

# John Thomson
Goalkeeper 1926-1931

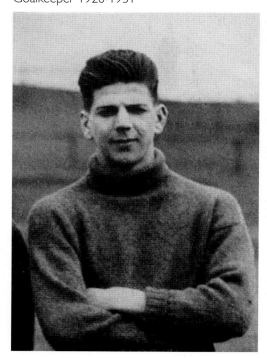

|                    | Appearances | Shut-outs |
|--------------------|-------------|-----------|
| League             | 163         | 57        |
| Scottish Cup       | 25          | 9         |
| Glasgow Cup        | 14          | 4         |
| Charity Cup        | 8           | 1         |
| Other Competitions | 2           | 1         |
| TOTAL              | 212         | 72        |

The boy from Fife became a martyr and legend in the history of Celtic FC. They said that there was nothing in football so graceful as the sight of John Thomson in full flight, 'gliding through the air like an eagle with the prey firmly clutched between his hands'. Born at 74 Balfour Street, Kirkcaldy, on 28 January 1909, he possessed from an early age all the lightning reflexes and cat-like leaps that go to make a great goalkeeper. Indeed, legend has it that at a children's party a small boy kicked a ball straight at an oil-lamp, but young Johnny dived and caught it just as tragedy seemed imminent.

A miner's son, John also went down the pit when barely fourteen, but his future always lay in the 'beautiful game'. He started with Bowhill juvenile sides West End and Rovers, and shortly afterwards stepped up to the junior ranks with Wellesley in 1925. The following year he was spotted by Celtic's chief scout Steve Callaghan, who produced a form from his pocket and held it against a telegraph pole for support, while Thomson signed on for a fee of £10. On becoming a Celt, Johnny took up digs with a great old lady at 618 Gallowgate, who looked after all the young players from out of Glasgow. He soon became a fearless custodian, who won over the hearts of every football fan as a true sportsman and well-mannered gentleman.

His ballet dancer-like agility captivated the imagination of spectators everywhere. A mere fortnight after his eighteenth birthday, he made his League debut against Dundee at Dens Park, with the teenage Thomson giving an immediate indication of how strong a character he possessed. During the first half of this game he made a slight error in judgement and fumbled a mishit cross to concede a 'soft' goal. Celtic thankfully recovered from this setback to record a 2–1 win. On the journey home, one of the directors, Tom Colgan, tried to console him about the slip-up, but was taken aback when the youngster gave a reply which was both frank and open. 'You'll not have to worry, sir. I have been taught never to make the same mistake twice. I'll be fine next week.' Two months later John Thomson had in his possession 'the most prized memento in the national game', a Scottish Cup winner's medal.

Johnny's superb performances were finally recognised by the selectors on 18 May 1930 when he starred in Scotland's comfortable 2–0 victory over France in Paris. Altogether he would represent Scotland and the Scottish League four times apiece.

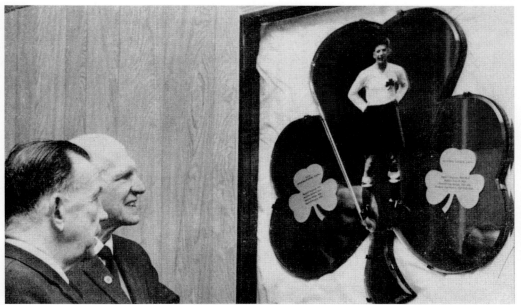

Chairman Bob Kelly and manager Jimmy McGrory look on in admiration at the John Thomson Shamrock memento at Celtic Park.

Arguably his greatest save came against Kilmarnock at Parkhead, when a 'Peerie' Cunningham swerving thunderbolt seemed certain to go for the right-hand post. Thomson dived for it in that direction. Almost on the instant he divined his mistake, the ball was travelling towards the left-hand post. Thomson twisted, literally in mid-air, hurled himself across the goal and got his fingers to the ball to turn it round the post. 'We stood open-mouthed', said Jimmy McGrory afterwards.

On 7 November 1928, at Villa Park, the Scottish League played a vastly superior Football League – which nevertheless won only by the odd goal in three. Time and again, Thomson stood alone before the English raiders. From one save, which brought him to his knees, the ball went to Ernie Hine, the fair-haired Leicester City inside right, who stood alone and unmarked 20 yards out. Hine's shot was one of those deliberate, tremendous, gathering-pace-as-they-go majestic shots such as only great inside forwards seem capable of producing. Thomson was still on his knees as it started on its way. Right from his knees

he rose, a gymnast's leap, arms outstretched and body arched. Somehow he got his fingers to the ball as it sped towards the underside of the bar, and flicked it over. The Villa Park grandstand echoed and trembled to a sustained outburst of applause which went on for minute after minute.

The following season, he kept the English forwards at bay as the Scottish League gained revenge at Ibrox by a 2–1 scoreline. In a League game against Airdrie on 5 February 1930, he sustained a fractured jaw and sore ribs. Thomson's bravery was such that his mother had once dreamt that he would be badly injured whilst keeping goal. Tragically his mother's nightmare became reality on 5 September 1931 at Ibrox, when he collided with Rangers' Sam English and died later that evening in the Victoria Infirmary of a depressed fracture of the skull. He had a deeply emotional funeral at Bowhill Cemetery, Cardenden. The following Saturday there was a touching scene before Celtic met Queen's Park at Parkhead. The players stood silent and the goal was left empty for two minutes whilst the 'Last Post' was sounded.

# Charlie Tully

Inside left, Outside left 1948-1959

|  | Appearances | Goals |
|---|---|---|
| League | 215 | 30 |
| Scottish Cup | 34 | 7 |
| League Cup | 69 | 8 |
| Glasgow Cup | 18 | 5 |
| Charity Cup | 14 | 2 |
| Other Competitions | 7 | 0 |
| TOTAL | 357 | 52 |

Charismatic and cheeky Charlie Tully was the 'Clown Prince of Paradise' throughout the 1950s. He arrived in Glasgow from Belfast in 1948 with a reputation for ball artistry and sublime skills – tricks as he called them – which prompted Belfast Celtic manager Elisha Scott to comment, 'Tricks? You should see him when he calls to collect his wages. That's the biggest trick of all.'

A mesmerising performance in his second Old Firm encounter on 25 September 1948 set Glesga' toon talking as he single-handedly ran Rangers' famous 'Iron Curtain' defence of Shaw, McColl, Young and Cox ragged with a quite devastating display of ball wizardry. The fans' tongues were kept wagging the following season, when an incident involving Tully and the Blues' favourite Sammy Cox almost incited a riot. At Ibrox, in full view of a packed Celtic end, Charlie was over-reaching himself in trying to control the ball inside the penalty area

when Cox appeared to kick him in the stomach. When the referee failed to award a penalty and waved play on, 'bottle parties' and fights broke out on the terracing. The upshot of all this commotion and hysteria saw the SFA reprimand both players and both clubs, but it was difficult to see what Tully had done wrong. The irrepressible Charlie with the forever turned up collar (forty years before Cantona came on the scene) had become a martyr-figure for many in Celtic's support.

With a sharp Irish wit softened by a disarming brogue, there was a charm and charisma about Tully which was forever being fuelled as fact often upstaged fiction. Within a few weeks, in May 1950, Charlie had shared a joke with American actor/comedian Danny Kaye, sung along with Bing Crosby on a cruise and been welcomed – as a member of the Celtic squad – to Rome by His Holiness Pope Pius XII. Back home they said that people in the Vatican that day were asking just who was that man with Charlie Tully!

On 4 October 1952, he made Windsor Park his stage and few spectators who saw him tease and tantalise the England defence are ever likely to forget the experience. Nor did Sir Alf Ramsey, then the full-back opposing him that afternoon. 'I gave Alf a tough day but he never attempted to rough it up. It was not his style;

The Celtic squad at the start of the 1956/57 season. Charlie Tully is the second player from the right, front row.

he always played his football fairly,' said Tully. Charlie scored both goals for Ireland in that 2–2 draw, one of them direct from a corner-kick with 'keeper Gil Merrick mesmerised by the in-swing. He amazingly topped this feat later that same season in a Scottish Cup tie at Brockville, when he netted twice direct from a retaken corner.

Celtic legend Tommy McInally used to meet up with Tully and his teammates every week and was always proud, to the point of vanity, about the fine Celtic team he played in. Charlie eventually riposted: 'Of course, you're right, Tommy, about these great players and their style of play. But, you must remember the fastest thing on earth in those days was a horse!' Tully, shrewd judge of the game though he was, always had an aversion to training. On lapping the track,

he once reflected: 'You don't learn how to play snooker by running round the table.'

Holder of 10 full caps for Northern Ireland and all the domestic club honours in Scotland, he subsequently managed Irish outfits Cork Hibs and Bangor. In 1967, when someone asked him if he merited a place in Celtic's 'Lisbon Lions' side, he replied: 'Sure, I could take the corners!' Charlie Tully died in his sleep on 27 July 1971, a few hours after leaving his lifelong friend Jackie Vernon. 'It was strange he should have gone out so peacefully. It was not his way of life,' wrote John Rafferty in *The Observer*. Huge crowds attended his funeral in Belfast and club officials and players travelled across the Irish Sea from Parkhead to pay their last respects to a truly great Celt.

# Willie Wallace
Forward 1966-1971

| | Appearances | Goals |
|---|---|---|
| League | 135 (6) | 88 |
| Scottish Cup | 25 (2) | 12 |
| League Cup | 31 (5) | 21 |
| Europe | 24 (2) | 13 |
| Other Competitions | 8 | 5 |
| TOTAL | 223 (15) | 139 |

William Wallace – what a wonderful name for a Scotsman – joined Celtic for £28,000 as a result of an ongoing financial dispute with Heart of Midlothian. A versatile forward and superb striker, 'Wispy' began his playing career with Stenhousemuir and had also starred for Raith Rovers before arriving at Parkhead midway through the successful 1966/67 campaign. Originally signed as cover for Stevie Chalmers, he replaced Joe McBride when the Govan goal machine received an ankle injury in December 1966.

A lively and elusive forward with a bustling style, Wallace was lethal in front of goal and obviously a marvellous asset to the club. Indeed, such a fine array of attacking attributes led manager Jock Stein to boast: 'He's a complete forward line in himself.' Willie scored twice in the European Cup semi-final first-leg win against Dukla Prague, and hit another brace in Celts' 1967 Scottish Cup final victory against Aberdeen. He capped a wonderful season by also playing in the memorable 3–2 triumph over the World Champions England at Wembley. His 18 goals in European competition (five with Hearts) was a Scottish record; and his goal in only eighteen seconds against Waterford is the club's quickest – and also its 100th in European soccer.

Transferred to Crystal Palace along with John Hughes for £30,000 in October 1971, he made 39 League appearances and netted 4 goals for the Selhurst Park club before returning home to join newly promoted Dumbarton in October 1972 for £10,000. At Boghead he teamed up with fellow ex-Celts Charlie Gallagher and John Cushley, and did his bit in providing the 'Sons of the Rock' with a respectable middle-of-the-table position in the top division the following season. The former vice-president of the Scottish Footballers' Association subsequently coached at Ross County and Dundee, and Sydney sides Apia and Leichhardt, leaving the latter in July 1982. Since 1984, Wallace has managed a sports shop in Mount Druitt, Australia.

|  | Appearances | Goals |
|---|---|---|
| League | 80 | 26 |
| Scottish Cup | 15 | 9 |
| League Cup | 10 | 2 |
| Glasgow Cup | 4 | 4 |
| Charity Cup | 5 | 1 |
| Other Competitions | 0 | 0 |
| TOTAL | 114 | 42 |

A nippy fast-raiding versatile forward, Jock Weir spent a relatively brief period at Parkhead, yet he will live forever in Celtic folklore as the man who scored a hat-trick to help the side avoid a possible relegation in 1948. Born at Fauldhouse on 20 October 1923, Weir began his career with Leith Renton before moving to Hibernian during the war. Transferred from the Easter Road club to Blackburn Rovers for £10,000 in January 1947, he still finished as Hibs' top scorer at the end of the 1946/47 season with 14 League goals and 23 in all competitions.

After a year in Lancashire, Celtic signed him on 17 February 1948, for a then Celts' record fee of £7,000. Celtic were looking for a thrustful forward with speed and power, and Jock filled the bill perfectly, making his debut in the most daunting of circumstances, a Scottish Cup tie against Motherwell before 55,231 spectators at Parkhead – a match which Celts won 1-0. Two months to the very day after his signing, he saved the club from the possibility of relegation by hitting a hat-trick at Dens Park to defeat Dundee 3–2 in the Bhoys' last League outing of the 1947/48 campaign.

The extrovert Weir had established his credentials and was soon a firm favourite with the Parkhead faithful. In his autobiography, *Passed to You*, Charlie Tully said of Weir: 'One for anybody's book. When they coined the word "gallus", they were thinking of Jock. He stayed at the Kenilworth Hotel for eighteen months at the club's expense. Whenever the boys were at a loose end, we used to go to the hotel and order a meal and put it on Jock's room number. I don't know how the club could afford it, or how Jock never tumbled to our game.'

A Scottish Cup winner with Celtic in 1951, Weir moved to Falkirk on 16 October 1952 and later that season scored for the 'Bairns' in the famous Scottish Cup tie at Brockville, in which Tully netted twice direct from a retaken corner. He later had brief spells at Llanelli and Dumbarton before retiring. Jock Weir died in early January 2003, aged seventy-nine.

# Peter Wilson
Right-half 1923-1934

|  | Appearances | Goals |
|---|---|---|
| League | 344 | 14 |
| Scottish Cup | 51 | 1 |
| Glasgow Cup | 30 | 0 |
| Charity Cup | 15 | 0 |
| Other Competitions | 1 | 0 |
| TOTAL | 441 | 15 |

Tall, quiet and unassuming when he first arrived at Parkhead, Peter Wilson hailed from the small Ayrshire village of Beith and joined Celtic in 1923 from a local amateur side. Something of a 'country bumpkin' and still wearing short knickerbocker trousers, he took some time to adjust to the hustle and bustle of city life in Glasgow, but on the football pitch he was soon at home as his stylish creative play gained him much acclaim. One of his specialities was an accurate long out-swinging ball to the far post. Wilson made his League debut for Celtic in a 1-0 victory at Motherwell on 13 February 1924 and went on to prove a splendid right-half who perfected his passing ability into such a fine art that he was said to stroke the ball, not merely kick it.

Red-faced, with laughing eyes, Peter also had bigger ears than most people. 'They catch so much wind they cost me a yard in speed,' he used to crack. He won the first of four international caps against Ireland on 27 February 1926. In his final appearance for Scotland, against England in 1933, he started the move that led to the winning goal scored by Jimmy McGrory, and 'The Hampden Roar' was born.

Transferred to Hibernian in the summer of 1934 after a dispute about re-signing terms, Peter observed: 'The Boss expects you to play like a genius on Saturdays, and to think like a half-wit on pay-days.' He turned out for the Bhoys at Paradise for the last time on 21 April 1934, in a 3–2 win over Dundee. With Celtic he gained a Championship badge in 1926 and Scottish Cup winner's medals in 1925, 1927, 1931 and 1933, and also made four appearances for the Scottish League.

He became Dunfermline Athletic's manager in 1938 and subsequently had a spell scouting for Derby County. Peter Wilson died in his native Beith in February 1983. Like a true Ayrshireman, he was a great Burns enthusiast and performer.

| | Appearances | Goals |
|---|---|---|
| League | 391 | 15 |
| Scottish Cup | 51 | 0 |
| Glasgow Cup | 39 | 2 |
| Charity Cup | 30 | 2 |
| Other Competitions | 11 | 0 |
| TOTAL | 522 | 19 |

All-time great 'Sunny Jim' Young was a member of two excellent Celtic sides – the six-in-a-row team of the late 1900s and the double winning eleven of the 1913/14 season. Fair-haired, tall and strapping. Kilmarnock-born James Young was an enthusiastic, hard-working right-half described by his manager Willie Maley as 'a man and a half in any team'. His endeavours on the football pitch made him a great favourite with the fans, who affectionately called him 'Sunny Jim' – a nickname which came from an advertisement for breakfast cereal, showing a vigorous figure in action with the words 'High o'er the fence leaps Sunny Jim, Force is the food which raises him.'

Young, whose pre-match ritual was to remove his false teeth before going on to the field, was brought to Celtic on a hunch, after a short trial with Bristol Rovers. Celtic were in the West Country trying to get Bob Muir, a former Kilmarnock outside right, to return home. When he agreed to do so, the homesick Young, who was standing nearby, remarked that he wished he was going too. Muir persuaded Celtic officials to bring Young back as well, and the club thus gained an outstanding personality and a splendid servant.

His commitment to the cause certainly could never be brought into question. On one memorable occasion in Berlin, when Celtic were touring Europe, 'Sunny Jim' chased a German defender around the field and out of the enclosure for having 'laid out' one of his team-mates. He made his debut for Celtic versus Hibernian in a goalless Charity Cup semi-final on 16 May 1903, and went on to collect a winners' medal that season. Previously with Stewarton and Shawbank, Young later skippered Celts to the League and cup double in 1914. He won numerous honours at club level, as well as a full Scotland cap against Ireland in Dublin in 1906, and six appearances for the Scottish League. Young's distinguished career ended after he twisted a knee in a League match at St Mirren on 19 August 1916, and although he played a few more games after that date, he never fully recovered and retired at the end of the season. He died tragically in a motorcycle accident at Hurlford in 1922, aged forty.

# Other Celtic titles published by Tempus

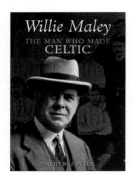

## Wille Maley  The Man Who Made Celtic
DAVID W. POTTER

Celtic owe almost everything to Willie Maley. He played in their first ever game in 1888 and won Scottish caps in 1893 before becoming Celtic's manager in 1897. He then set about building Celtic into the best team in Scotland and, from the beginning, envisaged the club as a powerful presence in world football. This book chronicles his playing career, the building of the great Edwardian Celtic team and the wealth of talent that he uncovered until his demission from office in 1940.

0 7524 3229 X

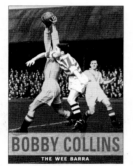

## Bobby Collins  The Wee Barra
DAVID SAFFER

Bobby Collins was world renowned for his fighting spirit and will to win for his team. Although small in stature, he was an inside forward and midfielder of awesome skill and considerable longevity: he played for Scotland for over fifteen years, scoring a goal for his country in the 1958 World Cup finals. Inspirational in Celtic's famous 7-1 thrashing of Rangers at Hampden, he was at Parkhead for over eight years before moving south. The author has worked closely with the player on this unique project.

0 7524 3176 5

## The Mighty Quinn  Jimmy Quinn, Celtic's First Goalscoring Hero
DAVID W. POTTER

Rising to prominence with his hat-trick in the Scottish Cup final of 1904 against Rangers, Jimmy Quinn became the spearhead of Willie Maley's great Edwardian side who won six League titles in a row. Making over 300 appearances and scoring 216 goals for his beloved Celtic, Quinn also became the hero of Scotland when in 1910 he almost single handedly beat England 2-0 to become the undisputed best player in Great Britain. Some of the very essence of Scottish football lies here in the story of Jimmy Quinn – a gratifying read for anyone with a love for the Scottish game.

0 7524 3460 8

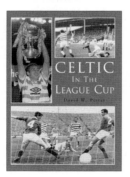

## Celtic In The League Cup
DAVID W. POTTER

From the start of the competition during the Second World War to the present day, the League Cup has provided a great deal of joy and a lot of frustration for Celtic fans. Having failed to make any real impact on the tournament for its first ten years as a peacetime competition, they have subsequently made up for the lost time. Surely the most memorable of these games, the 7-1 thrashing of Rangers in the 1957 final, must rate as one of the best matches of all time for any supporter of the Bhoys!

0 7524 2435 1

If you are interested in purchasing other books published by Tempus, or in case you have difficulty finding any Tempus books in your local bookshop, you can also place orders directly through our website

**www.tempus-publishing.com**